THE
LITTLE
BOOK
OF
DUBLIN

BRENDAN NOLAN

The History Press Ireland

For Martin, a brother

First published 2014

The History Press Ireland
50 City Quay
Dublin 2
Ireland
www.thehistorypress.ie

British Library Cataloguing in Publication Data.
A catalogue record for this book is available from the British Library.

ISBN 978 1 84588 815 2

Production managed by Jellyfish
Printed in Malta by Melita Press

CONTENTS

ACKNOWLEDGEMENTS

Thanks to all Dubliners who went before me, whether native born, of extraction, or by inclination, and to all who will come after me to live in this wonderful, mythical, mad place. Not forgetting Maggie, May, Rita, Alison, Rachel, Josh, Holly, Leo and Luci.

INTRODUCTION

'What's the craic?' is a question put by Dubliners to elicit information on anything from personal wellbeing to economic prospects, both local and global. It's up to you how you'd like to respond.

Ptolemy, the Alexandrian geographer, might have wondered what the craic was when he made mention of Dublin as a maritime city in the second century on a map he was fooling with at the time. After that, nothing much happened for about six centuries, until lads from Scandinavia were marauding about the place in their longboats and they too wondered about Dublin Bay. They saw in it a nice sheltered haven for seafarers and a sound strategic site for trade, not to mention the chance to head ashore and stretch their legs for a while.

And so it came to pass that in the ninth century the Norsemen, or Vikings, established a settlement at a deep, dark pool on the Liffey that became known as the Black Pool or Dubh Linn (Dublin). The settlement was somewhere below where Christ Church Cathedral now stands upon the hill above the modern Liffey. Not far from there someone developed a ford across part of the river that is now Church Street Bridge, or Father Matthew Bridge, or whatever you wish to call it yourself. This was known as the hurdle ford, so Dubh Linn became known as Baile Átha Cliath, the town of the hurdle ford, which name it keeps in Irish. Thus Dublin has two names, one for either tongue: great craic, as lost travellers must often have said when wondering where they were.

Ireland was not devoid of people before this; there were lots of clans about the place, and few paid any attention to these new lads. That is until they started to take prisoners and sell them off to their cousins as slaves in other countries and to chase the local maidens. Up to then, the Irish were too busy having differences of opinion among themselves to bother about the invaders and their long boats pulled up on the shore. Just to confuse matters more, as the years passed, the Norsemen married into powerful Irish clans and everyone became cousins.

Nonetheless, the Danes, as they were known as by then, were defeated in the Battle of Clontarf, near Dublin, in 1014 under the leadership of the Irish warrior king, Brian Boru. Some left Ireland after this, while some stayed and nursed their grievances with the wife's family and said there was no craic left in Dublin anymore.

However, matters grew worse in 1170 with the appearance of the Anglo-Normans, who had invaded through Wexford the previous year and seized control of the town, sending the Norsemen north of the river to set up home at Oxmanstown, near to where the Phoenix Park is now laid out. The Normans settled in and built some nice new walls around Dublin. In the early thirteenth century they built a castle, officially securing Dublin as an English holding.

For seven centuries Dublin was to remain a seat and symbol of British authority until a successful War of Independence in the twentieth century sent the invader home to look for craic in his own country. That war had its beginnings on O'Connell Street in the heart of Dublin, in 1916, when the rebels read a proclamation of independence, and, with their few arms, defied an empire that was already at war in Europe. The ensuing battle wrecked the centre of the city when English artillery was used to dislodge the fighters.

But before that disagreement, eighteenth-century Ireland had seen peace, and improvements in agriculture. Many landlords lived in fine houses in Dublin and the city prospered, not least in the fabric of the city. New residential terraces were laid out and streets were widened to accommodate fine carriages and the commerce of a thriving city of the empire. Georgian houses and squares spread about the city with their fine facades and mews houses to the rear, which doubled as stables and carriage houses and living accommodation for staff.

Not all was wine and roses for the inhabitants of the city, however, for older clay houses were home to people of little substance, or put another way: those who had no arse in their trousers. Streets were narrow and animals wandered the streets as casually as humans; such latitude was reflected in the heavy smells that greeted a visitor, everywhere. Frequent official decrees were issued to take the animals off the streets, if you please, or the bailiffs would be free to seize such livestock as were causing nuisance and could be caught.

Nonetheless, for the wealthy, life was good and, as in modern times, property owners vied with one another to show excess in fashion and accommodation. However, Georgian glory was not to last.

Once the Irish parliament, whose home was on College Green opposite Trinity College, voted itself out of business and joined in a union with Westminster in 1800, the great Georgian houses began to empty of the rich and powerful. In the century that followed, the Georgian terraces of large-roomed houses became sub-divided by exploitative landlords and inexorably turned into slum dwellings. Not such good craic for those families of several generations trying to live with some dignity in a single room. By the mid-twentieth century some old buildings had begun to fall down from neglect, with consequent loss of life to the unfortunates living inside. The city council built housing estates in the suburbs and re-housed the most vulnerable of the city's needy.

However, no amount of boom or bust could keep a good story or song down for long and the Irish Literary Revival of the nineteenth and twentieth century saw many artists come to the fore; mostly in the spoken or transcribed word – the art form most beloved of the Irish. Revival began with a national resurgence of interest in the Irish language and Irish culture, including folklore, sports, music and arts. It was to blossom into a flowering of great writing both for the page and the stage, arising from a strong tradition of oral storytelling, or the craic, as some would have it.

Dublin produced three Nobel Laureates in literature: Yeats, Shaw and Beckett, with James Joyce as a spare, for he was not awarded a prize at all, even though Becket had worked with Joyce for a while. Seamus Heaney, the poet from Derry, another Nobel Laureate, lived by the sea in Sandymount, Dublin Bay in his final years.

The Man Booker literary prize was won by Iris Murdoch from Phibsborough (1978), Roddy Doyle (1993), John Banville (2005) and Anne Enright (2007): all Dubliners. Dublin also produced great playwrights: Seán O'Casey, Brendan Behan, George Bernard Shaw, Richard Brinsley Sheridan, John Millington Synge, Oscar Wilde, William Butler Yeats, Hugh Leonard, Bernard Farrell, Peter Sheridan, Jim Sheridan, Sebastian Barry and many more.

In 2010, it became a UNESCO City of Literature and now has so many festivals that you are never far from the next one. In music, Dublin has hosted the Eurovision song contest, on six occasions. The city also introduced *Riverdance* to the world, as the 1994 Eurovision Song Contest interval act. The winners that year were Dubliner Paul Harrington and Donegal man Charlie McGettigan, with Rock 'n' Roll Kids. Lots of craic ensued, as everyone knows.

Dublin saw an influx of new invaders after the EU enlarged itself in 2004, when Ireland held the EU Presidency and all the EU leaders gathered in Farmleigh beside Phoenix Park for the craic. The new invaders were people coming for a better life. Some stayed, some went home again; many others took citizenship and their children now sport Dublin accents. No matter the colour of their skin or their features, for the new Irish all know what the craic is in Dublin. And in Dublin that is all that matters.

Dublin has a seaside to enjoy and a national park – Phoenix Park – that is the biggest walled park in Europe, bigger than Central Park and certainly bigger than any park in London. Dublin has mountains in its southern suburbs and flat farmland to the west and north, not forgetting a pair of canals encircling the city.

On weekend nights, streets in Temple Bar are alive with people searching for craic and wandering from place to place enjoying traditional Dublin food, music and Irish dancing. Or just telling stories. Nightclubs supply a concoction of sounds to satisfy all ears. Dublin has many dedicated gay venues and accommodation in the city centre, located on a strip from Capel Street, north of the river, to George's Street on the south, via Parliament Street and Temple Bar.

The Globalization and World Cities Research Network ranks Dublin among the top thirty cities in the world. But Dubliners knew that already.

Dublin is at once a modern centre of education, the arts, administration, economy and industry. It is a city where its people know the value of everything and the enjoyment that is to be had in their city of choice. Ptolemy knew that, as did the Vikings and the Normans and all those who came for the craic and stayed for the life that is Dublin.

Enjoy.

Brendan Nolan
www.irishfolktales.com

1

FAMOUS FACES

SWIFT EATING CHILDREN

Jonathan Swift wrote *Gulliver's Travels* as a political satire of his time. However, children took it at face value and it has been a classic of children's literature ever since. Swift, in similar vein, also wrote *A Modest Proposal* in which he put forward a plan to cannibalise children for profit and as an alternative way of dealing with starvation in Ireland. Suffice it to say, this plan has not been proceeded with, yet.

Swift was born in Hoey's Court a few weeks before Christmas of 1667. As an adult, Swift moved to England to work as secretary first for Sir William Temple and then the Earl of Berkeley but in 1713 he accepted a position at the Deanery of St Patrick's. On the eve of his departure for Dublin, Vanessa, who had studied with him and was then aged 23, confessed her love for him. Swift was surprised but it seems unmoved at her declaration for he returned home to Dublin without her.

A few years later, Vanessa and her sister took up residence at Celbridge, near Dublin. By now, Swift was paying attention to Esther Johnston, whom he nicknamed Stella, to whom, some say, he was secretly married in 1716. However, it is also said that he tired of Stella and cast his eyes upon his former student Vanessa instead, which caused disruptions. Vanessa, hearing rumours about Stella, wrote to her to inquire the nature of her claims upon the good dean. Stella showed the letter to Swift, who rode out to Celbridge to see Vanessa. He flung her letter to Stella on the table and walked out of the house without a word, bitter or sweet. Three weeks later, Vanessa died of a broken heart aged 37, which was a bit extreme, some say.

Jonathan Swift was Dean of St Patrick's Cathedral from 1713 until his death in 1745 at the age of 77, which was very old for that time. The cathedral has in its possession early editions of his writings, a pair of his death masks, though he died only once, and a cast of the good man's skull.

Swift was troubled by imbalance and noises in his ears in later years. Together with a stroke in 1742, his condition led many to declare him mad. However, 90 years after he died, Swift's body was exhumed and examined by Oscar Wilde's father, Sir William Wilde, a prominent physician. He discovered that Swift had a loose bone in his inner ear, and this is what had been at the root of many of the dead man's problems.

Coincidentally, Swift left money in his will to found St Patrick's Hospital, a hospital for treating those with mental illness; it still exists today, not far from the road to Celbridge where Swift would have travelled out to see Vanessa.

THE QUARE ON THE SQUARE

Oscar Wilde once said that, 'A man can be happy with any woman as long as he does not love her'. He was to attempt to prove his theory when he married Constance Lloyd, daughter of Horace Lloyd, a wealthy Queen's Counsel. The couple had two sons, Cyril (1885) and Vyvyan (1886).

Oscar Fingal O'Flahertie Wills Wilde, Irish writer and poet, became one of London's most popular playwrights in the early 1890s, before being imprisoned for homosexual activity. He also wrote a collection of children's stories, *The Happy Prince and Other Tales*, still told to children today.

In death, no less than in life, Dublin-born Wilde attracts attention. He passed away in 1900 and was initially buried in the Cimetière de Bagneux outside Paris in 1909, before his remains were moved to Père Lachaise Cemetery, inside the city. His tomb was designed by Sir Jacob Epstein, whose original modernist angel on the tomb was complete with male genitalia. However, someone stole Wilde's token private parts and their whereabouts never became known. Nonetheless, in 2000, a silver prosthesis was made to replace them. In 2011, the tomb was cleaned of lipstick marks left there by admirers and a glass barrier was installed to prevent further marks or damage.

At the height of his fame and success, Wilde prosecuted the Marquess of Queensberry, the father of Wilde's lover Lord Alfred Douglas, for libel. However, matters for Wilde took a turn for the worse when the trial led to his own arrest and trial for gross indecency with other men. Wilde was convicted and imprisoned for two years' hard labour. Ever the writer, he wrote *De Profundis* while incarcerated. It began as a letter to Douglas recalling their time together, but grew to be a larger work than simply a recall of times past. Upon his release, Wilde immediately left for France, never to return to Ireland or Britain. He died in destitution in Paris at the age of 46.

Wilde is commemorated in his native Dublin by a colourful reclining figure atop a huge 35-tonne quartz rock on the corner of Merrion Square, not far from his birthplace on Westland Row. Dubliners well-known for their turn of phrase have renamed the monument 'The Quare on the Square'.

THE PLAYBOY SYNGE

According to John Millington Synge the tramp in Ireland is little troubled by the laws, and lives in out-of-door conditions that keep him in good humour and fine bodily health. Synge was once told by a tramp he met that although he was born in Dublin, he had travelled a great deal and had been in Paris and Rome and seen Pope Leo XIII.

Rathfarnham-born Synge (b. 16 April 1871) was a playwright, poet, prose writer and collector of folklore. A key figure in the Irish Literary Revival of the early twentieth century, he was one of the co-founders of the Abbey Theatre, along with his friend the poet and playwright W.B. Yeats.

Synge's play *The Playboy of the Western World* caused riots in Dublin during its opening run at the Abbey Theatre in January 1907. The riots were stirred up by nationalists who viewed the contents of the play as an offence to public morals and an insult to Ireland. When a significant portion of the crowd rioted, the remainder of the play was acted out in dumb show. Crossing the Atlantic did not do much for the mood of the audience either. On opening night in New York in 1911, hecklers booed, hissed and threw vegetables and stink bombs, while men scuffled in the aisles.

The stylised realism of his writing about Irish rural life, especially in Wicklow, Kerry, the Aran Islands and the West was to influence a great many emerging playwrights in Ireland for many years, both rural and urban. Samuel Beckett was a frequent visitor when Synge's plays were performed.

Synge died of Hodgkin's disease, which was untreatable at the time, just weeks short of his 38th birthday. He was attempting to complete his final play, *Deirdre of the Sorrows*, at the time of his passing.

JAMES JOYCE, SINGER AND CINEMA OWNER

The James Joyce Bridge crosses the Liffey from Usher's Island to Blackhall Place to commemorate the Dublin writer. Opened to motor traffic on 16 June 2003 (Bloomsday), it touches land at 15 Usher's Island, where Joyce's short story *The Dead*, from his collection *Dubliners*, is set. Many enthusiastic young boys who had never met Joyce would climb to the top of the bridge to slide down the steel arches beside the passing traffic, until the Garda had to ask local parents to intervene.

Rathgar-born Joyce left Ireland in his early twenties to live, at one time or another, in Trieste, Paris and Zurich. However, he said: 'I always write about Dublin, because if I can get to the heart of Dublin I can get to the heart of all the cities of the world.'

Joyce is best known for his book *Ulysses* (1922), in which the episodes of Homer's Odyssey are paralleled in an array of contrasting literary styles. The entire book takes place in Dublin on 16 June 1904; the date Joyce and his future wife Nora Barnacle first stepped out together. It was also the inspiration for Bloomsday (named after the central character in *Ulysses*, Leopold Bloom), which is celebrated in Dublin on 16 June each year; a commemoration of something that did not happen. It was fictitious. A novel.

During Bloomsday, aficionados dress in Edwardian attire and partake of a breakfast as close as possible to the original meal consumed by Leopold Bloom. That is: the inner organs of beasts and fowls, thick giblet soup, nutty gizzards, a stuffed roast heart, liver slices fried with crust crumbs, fried hencods' roes and grilled mutton kidneys.

Apart from being a writer of books, Joyce was an accomplished tenor and won the bronze medal in the 1904 Feis Ceoil. In 1909, with the backing of some cinema owners and businessmen, the 27-year-old Joyce launched Ireland's first cinema – the 600-seat Volta Cinematograph at 45 Mary Street, now part of a department store. However, the venture diminished when Joyce left Dublin for Trieste once more.

European copyright on all Joyce's work expired on 1 January 2012, seventy years after the writer's death. This includes *Finnegans Wake*, *Ulysses*, *Dubliners* and *A Portrait of the Artist as a Young Man*, which are now technically in the public domain.

O'CASEY AT WAR

Playwright Sean O'Casey was born at 85 Upper Dorset Street, which at the time was not in the middle of the working-class society in which many of his plays are set. He was born into a lower-middle-class Irish Protestant family, but his father died when he was a child and, consequently, the family became progressively poorer. With only three years of formal schooling, and suffering from poor eyesight, the young O'Casey educated himself by reading.

O'Casey started work at the age of 14, mostly undertaking manual labour, in common with a great many other children once primary school was completed. Later on, he learned Irish and took up the uilleann pipes. In 1910, he was a founder member of the St Laurence O'Toole Pipe Band, a band that provided music to many of the nationalist moments during the War of Independence of the early twentieth century. The band's headquarters on Seville Place was raided by the army and police many times in this period.

O'Casey's play *The Frost in the Flower* was commissioned by the Saint Laurence O'Toole National Club in 1918. His 1920 play *The Plough and the Stars* staged at the Abbey Theatre met with protests from audience members, who decided to riot rather than see any more of the play. His play *The Drums of Father Ned* was also met with protest. It was supposed to be performed at the 1958 Dublin Theatre Festival, but the Catholic Archbishop of Dublin, John Charles McQuaid, who wielded huge influence at the time, refused to give his blessing to it. O'Casey's was not the only play to receive criticism – a dramatisation of James Joyce's *Ulysses* was also dropped. In protest, Samuel Beckett withdrew a play of his that was also scheduled to be performed in that year's festival.

In his declining years O'Casey urged younger writers not to be 'afraid of life's full-throated shouting, afraid of its venom, suspicious of its gentleness, its valour, its pain and its rowdiness'.

His three major plays are: *The Shadow of a Gunman*, *Juno and the Paycock* and *The Plough and the Stars*. All are tragicomedies set in the slums of Dublin during a time of war and revolution.

A TERRIBLE BEAUTY

When Sandymount-born William Butler Yeats accepted an invitation to become a member of the new Irish Senate, he served for six years from 1922 and chaired a committee, overseeing the selection of designs for the new currency of Ireland.

A proposal to feature Christian saints on the new coins was ruled out, as it was thought the coins would be made into religious medals by the more devout patriots of the day. Instead, the currency committee said the Irish harp would be used as the national symbol on coins, with the reverse featuring a series of animals important to Ireland's agricultural economy at the time. It led to coin tossers calling heads or harps as they awaited the spin of a coin to settle matters.

The first coins of the Irish Free State were made in the Royal Mint in London. Many of the gods depicted on Dublin's Custom House appeared on the original Sir John Lavery Irish banknotes of the new State. The likeness of Lavery's wife, Lady Hazel Lavery, appeared on banknotes of the Republic of Ireland for much of the twentieth century.

During a 1925 Senate debate on divorce legislation, Yeats said:

> Many would welcome a very simple solution, namely, that the Catholic members should remain absent when a Bill of Divorce was brought before the House that concerned Protestants and non-Catholics only, and that it would be left to the Protestant members, or some Committee appointed by those Protestant members, to be dealt with. I think it would be the first instinct of the members of both Houses to adopt some such solution and it is obvious, I think, that from every point of view of national policy and national reputation that would be a wise policy.

Admirable as his policy was, it was not agreed to.

Yeats was later asked by the chairman of the Seanad, Lord Glenavy, if he might leave the dead alone. Yeats had used Daniel O'Connell, Charles Stewart Parnell and Admiral Lord Nelson as reference points on extramarital behaviour before he was called to attention. All three dead men were commemorated with public statues on O'Connell Street, Dublin's main thoroughfare. Just two remain: O'Connell and Parnell, who occupy each end of the street. Nelson was blown down in 1966 by republican activists, clearing the street for a fiftieth commemoration of the Easter Rising of 1916.

'Easter, 1916', a poem by W.B. Yeats, described the poet's torn emotions regarding the events of the Easter Rising against British rule on Easter Monday, 24 April 1916. The line: 'A Terrible Beauty is Born', is oft quoted from the poem.

A NOBEL CALLING

Dublin has so far had three Nobel Laureates in Literature: William Butler Yeats, George Bernard Shaw and Samuel Beckett. James Joyce was not one of them. Alfred Bernhard Nobel – whose legacy, as his name suggests, is the Nobel Prize – invented dynamite and was a major manufacturer of armaments. After his death, he left a few bob for peace prizes and the like to be awarded in his name.

William Butler Yeats was awarded the 1923 Nobel Prize for Literature, 'for his always inspired poetry, which in a highly artistic form gives expression to the spirit of a whole nation'. Yeats famously told a rioting audience from the stage at the Abbey Theatre's 1926 production of Sean O'Casey's *The Plough and the Stars*: 'You have disgraced yourselves again. This is O'Casey's apotheosis.' Dubliners have disgraced themselves ever since, as opportunity arose.

George Bernard Shaw, the 1925 winner, received his Prize a year late, in 1926. For during the selection process in 1925, the Nobel Committee decided that none of the year's nominations met the criteria outlined in the will of Alfred Nobel. Shaw, therefore, confusingly received his Nobel Prize for 1925 in 1926 for his work which the Committee said was: 'marked by both idealism and humanity, its stimulating satire often being infused with a singular poetic beauty.'

Samuel Beckett, the 1969 Nobel prizewinner, was denounced as a 'bawd and blasphemer' by Oliver St John Gogarty's counsel when, in his thirties, the younger Beckett gave evidence on behalf of William Sinclair (his late uncle-by-marriage) in a libel case against Gogarty for words used about the uncle and his twin brother Harry Sinclair in Gogarty's 1935 book *As I Was Going Down Sackville Street*. The book is described as a semi-fictional memoir, telling the story of Gogarty's Dublin through a series of interconnected anecdotes and lively characters sketches. Gogarty lost and was ordered to pay £900 in damages, plus court costs.

In 2013, the Irish Naval service declared that two new ships would be named the LE *Samuel Beckett* (delivery 1914) and the LE *James Joyce* (delivery 1915). They did not say if Yeats or Shaw would be so remembered. Still, they did get a medal off the fella that invented dynamite, so there was that.

BANNED FOR WRITING

When a writer's work was banned under the Censorship of Publications Act, shopkeepers would not stock the writer's next book for fear it would also be banned. The Act provided for the banning of publications on three grounds: if they were in general tendency indecent or obscene; if they devoted an unduly large proportion of space to the publication of matter relating to crime; or they advocated the unnatural prevention of conception or the procurement of abortion or miscarriage. Almost all writers of note were banned at one time or another under this strict censorship regime. In 1967 changes were made so that the period for which a book could be banned was limited to twelve years.

Lee Dunne from Rathmines was the most banned writer in Ireland. One of Dunne's titles, *Paddy Maguire is Dead*, was banned in Ireland in 1972 before finally being published in his native country thirty-four years later in 2006 (although it was on open sale in Britain throughout this time). Interestingly, when the first two parts of Lee Dunne's Paddy Maguire trilogy about a womanising alcoholic were published in hardback, there was no response from the censors; however, when Dunne insisted the final part be published in paperback at one seventh the selling price of the hardback, and, therefore, accessible to more people, the book was banned. In response to the ban, Dunne commented: '*Paddy Maguire is Dead* is the most important book on alcoholism ever to come out of Ireland. It's a sexy book but it's a moral book. Rather than being didactic, the guy picks up the tag at the end, the morality is there. I thought it was a joke that it was banned.' Six more Dunne titles were banned after that: *Midnight Cabbie*,

The Day of the Cabbie, *The Cabbie who Came in from the Cold*, *The Virgin Cabbie* and *The Cabfather*.

Dunne adapted the Paddy Maguire saga for the stage and offered it as dinner theatre in a Dublin hotel, where it ran to full houses and commercial success for several years while the book version remained banned.

No book has been banned since 2003, which says everything about life in twenty-first-century Ireland.

TOE TO TOE

Christy Brown was a Dublin writer and painter who was able to write or type only with the toes of one foot. He was born into a large family in North King Street, in 1932, but the family was re-housed in Kimmage by the city council when it built large tracts of housing on the outskirts of the city.

My Left Foot, the Academy Award-winning film of the book, might never have been made by Dublin film director Jim Sheridan were it not for the tenacity of Brown's family in keeping Brown at home, even though doctors wanted to commit him to hospital, as they had diagnosed severe cerebral palsy, which left him almost entirely paralysed by spasticity. Dialogue from the film, 'Let Christy take it', when a prone Christy shoots a penalty with devastating consequences for the other team, became a Dublin catchphrase when decisiveness against great odds was required.

SMOKING MATTRESS

Fellow writer Brendan Behan was born on Russell Street, not far away from Christy Brown, and, coincidentally, also moved with his family to Kimmage, where Behan said the natives ate their children, so far was it from civilization – though there was hardly more than 10km between the city home and the suburban house.

Behan could talk for Ireland. Having joined the IRA at the age of 16 and being arrested in Britain, he served time in a borstal institution in England and in prison in Ireland, about which he said: 'The Bible was a consolation to a fellow alone in the old cell. The lovely thin paper with a bit of mattress stuffing in it, if you could get a match, was as good a smoke as I ever tasted.' Of his revolutionary activities he remarked: 'When I came back to Dublin I was court-martialled in my absence and sentenced to death in my absence, so I said they could shoot me in my absence.'

The Quare Fellow, Behan's first play, was produced in 1954 in Dublin. In 1958, Behan's play in the Irish language *An Giall* was performed at Dublin's Damer Theatre.

Behan's uncle, Peadar Kearney, wrote the Irish National Anthem, 'Amhrán na bhFiann' ('The Soldier's Song'). A housepainter by trade, Kearney taught night classes in Irish and numbered playwright Sean O'Casey among his pupils. He worked for the National Theatre Society, which was co-founded by W.B. Yeats.

2

SAINTS AND SINNERS

TAKE ME UP TO MONTO

Wherever there are large concentrations of males with money to spend there will be red-light ladies willing to relieve them of their cash.

Montgomery Street, which lay east of O'Connell Street, became the hub of a red-light area in Dublin, which inevitably attracted the nickname of the Monto. It was reputed to be the biggest red-light district in Europe in its heyday. It sprawled roughly an area surrounded by modern-day Talbot Street, Amiens Street, Gardiner Street and Seán McDermott Street and was adjacent to major railway terminals and the busy docks of Dublin. From the 1860s until the 1900s, as many as 1,600 prostitutes – some fresh faced, some wretched – were working there.

Many of the soldiers of the British Army who were stationed in Dublin barracks made a ready market for the whores of Dublin. So enthusiastically did these liaisons proceed that at any given time many of the soldiers were off duty, suffering from the sickness of sin. Some male callers would walk into the Monto to avail of services and some would be enticed in fashionable parts of the city by girls in horse-drawn carriages, dressed in finery supplied by the controlling madams. In the Circe chapter of James Joyce's *Ulysses* Monto is disguised as Nighttown, where the central protagonists, Leopold Bloom and Stephen Dedalus, visit a brothel together. Furthermore, according to popular legend, Prince Albert Edward (later King Edward VII) left more than his calling card there.

When girls became too old or were stricken by disease they were tossed out on the street by the madams in favour of new faces. Some went to The Lock hospitals, which specialised in the treatment of sexually transmitted disease. Hopelessly affected women were transferred from the hospital to a Lock prison and kept there until their life ended, naturally or assisted, sooner or later.

In 1925, a successful campaign was launched against the Monto by well-meaning citizens, forcing its closure.

LEGION OF MARY AT WAR WITH THE DEVIL

Frank Duff, founder of the Legion of Mary, was born at 97 Phibsboro Road, Dublin on 7 June 1889. A plaque on the front of the building now marks the spot.

Duff is best known for founding the Legion, and for bringing attention to the role of the laity during the Second Vatican Council of the Roman Catholic Church in the 1960s. Duff founded the Legion of Mary, a lay apostolic organisation operating under ecclesiastical guidance, on 7 September 1921. Its purpose, so it says, is the spiritual development of its members and advancing the reign of Christ through Mary. Members are guided by the tenets of the Handbook of the Legion of Mary, a great deal of which was penned by Duff himself. Its opening paragraph states:

> The Legion of Mary is an Association of Catholics who, with the sanction of the Church and under the powerful leadership of Mary Immaculate, Mediatrix of all Graces (who is fair as the moon, bright as the sun, and – to Satan and his legionaries – terrible as an army set in battle array), have formed themselves into a Legion for service in the warfare which is perpetually waged by the Church against the world and its evil powers.

Duff was convinced that without exception all are called to be saints, and that through Christian faith all persons have available the means necessary to attain such sainthood.

Between active and auxiliary members there are reportedly between 3 and 10 million members (legionnaires) worldwide, depending on who is counting. Surprisingly, for a Christian lay organisation, the Legion is modelled on the military chain of command of the Ancient Roman Army, starting with the praesidium as its smallest unit. The Concilium is the highest level; it has its seat in Dublin and control over all of the Legion, wherever it may be at any time.

Since Duff's death at the age of 91 on 7 November 1980, his own cause for canonisation has been advanced by admirers. An official petition to introduce the cause for the beatification of Duff was accepted and signed by the then Archbishop of Dublin, Cardinal Desmond Connell in July 1996. Duff is now known under the title Servant of God and the many members of the Legion have been asked to pray for his canonisation.

A MAN OF MANY PARTS
ST LAWRENCE O'TOOLE

St Lawrence O'Toole is one of two official patron saints of Dublin, the other being St Kevin. Two more dead souls may be added to the list if petitions are successful: Frank Duff, founder of the Legion of Mary; and Matt Talbot, a religious zealot or a born saint, depending on your point of view.

St Lawrence O'Toole, who rattled about the place from 1128 to 1180, has his official feast day on 14 November. He was born a son of Murtagh, Chief of the Murrays, in Castledermot, County Kildare.

Career paths were different in those days. Young O'Toole was taken hostage at age 10 by King Dermot McMurrogh of Leinster and then surrendered to the Bishop of Glendalough, where Lawrence became a monk, without going home to Kildare to take up his interrupted life there. By 1161, he had gotten on well enough to be named Archbishop of Dublin. He wore a hair shirt and spent forty days every year retreating and praying in St Kevin's cave in Glendalough, so he must have been pious.

This consecration of a native-born Irishman marked the passing away of Danish supremacy in Dublin's ecclesiastical circles. Later on, in 1180, after a mission to King Henry II of England, Lawrence headed to Normandy in France where, at Eu, his travels on this earth ended, at least for a while.

Lawrence was canonized in 1225, after reports of miracles at his tomb, and has been a saint ever since. His skull was interred at a church in Lancashire, but his bones disappeared during the Reformation. They have not, as yet, turned up.

Furthermore, his preserved heart, which was kept in Dublin's Christ Church Cathedral and inspired pilgrimages to it since medieval times, was stolen in March 2012 by persons unknown, for reasons also unknown.

GETTING LUCKY

As a largely Roman Catholic country, people lived under the strictures of Church teaching when it came to contraception. You could be a sinner and be in big trouble, morally, if you did not follow the correct path. The 1930 Encyclical (Papal Directive) Casti Connubii specified that:

> ... any use whatsoever of matrimony exercised in such a way that the act is deliberately frustrated in its natural power to generate life is an offence against the law of God and of nature, and those who indulge in such are branded with the guilt of a grave sin.

For purposes of clarification, that was followed by Humanae Vitae in 1968, after the contraceptive pill had been developed, which decreed that artificial contraception in all forms was immoral and should not be used.

Owning and using contraceptive devices and pills was not illegal but they could not be sold or imported legally after a 1935 Act prohibited such carry-on. But while such devices could not be offered for sale, a client could make an offer to buy. Some people made donations to family planning associations to obtain contraception as a gift – it was like buying yourself a present. This arrangement often led to queues of people forming on Cathal Brugha Street, off O'Connell Street, and other places, while people made offers on supplies for the weekend in designated outlets.

In 1971, in an attempt to make a nonsense of the law, Irish feminists travelled to Belfast by rail and made their return to

Dublin laden with contraceptive devices, as technically Belfast is in the United Kingdom where contraceptives could legally be bought and sold.

In 1973, the Supreme Court affirmed that there was a constitutional right to marital privacy, which also allowed for the use of contraceptives; but they still could not be sold openly. Five years later, the future taoiseach and adulterer Charles Haughey TD as Minister for Health steered an Act into law whereby contraceptives could only be dispensed by a pharmacist on the presentation of a valid medical prescription from a practising doctor.

However, since 2010 contraceptives of all sorts are widely available, legally, and many Dublin hotspots provide condoms through dispensing machines for their patrons. Prices vary, from the eminently sensible to the daft. But, as always, you pays your moneys and you takes your chances.

GAY RIGHTS

It was against the law to engage in homosexuality in Ireland and, therefore, it was a sin until 23 June 1993, when a Bill to decriminalise homosexuality passed all stages in the Irish parliament, the Dáil. On the following day, gay people took part in the 1993 Dublin Pride March, celebrating their open sexuality. The nineteenth-century laws had not countenanced homosexual activity between women, so they only applied to males.

In 1983 Dublin resident Senator David Norris took a constitutional case against the laws in Ireland, which failed at the Supreme Court. However, he then successfully appealed to the European Court of Human Rights, where his lead counsel was Mary Robinson, later to become the first woman president of Ireland.

The passing of all stages of the Criminal Law (Sexual Offences) Bill 1993 followed a strong campaign by GLEN (the Gay and Lesbian Equality Network), the ICCL (Irish Council for Civil Liberties), the Trade Union movement, and others, for a change in the law. The ruling Fianna Fáil/Labour coalition government agreed to bring forward the Bill, which established an equal age of consent (17 years of age) for homosexual and heterosexual humans alike.

In 1979 the newly established NGF (National Gay Federation) leased a building, called the Hirschfeld Centre, in the underdeveloped Temple Bar area of Dublin. The community centre was the first full-time gay and lesbian venue in Ireland. It housed a meeting space, a youth group, a café and a small cinema and film club. It also ran discos at the weekend where lesbian, gay, bisexual and transgendered people socialised. Furthermore, it provided a telephone counselling service, in consultation with the Samaritans, and spearheaded a campaign among gay people in the fight against the AIDS epidemic. It closed after a fire on the premises in 1987.

A NATURAL BORN KILLER AT THE PICTURES

Most parishes in Dublin had its own local cinema in a pre-television age. But, national film censorship under the 1923 Censorship of Films Act saw films that were considered to be indecent, obscene, blasphemous or subversive of public morality, being banned or cut. A national film censor was appointed, who signed a certificate that had to be shown before all screenings of every film to a public audience (there have been nine film censors, to date, all male). Moreover, censorship of films allowed for no grading, so, until 1965, all pictures had to be suitable for all ages, from the babe in arms to the pipe-sucking ancient in the back row. This led to wholesale massacres of plot sense and pivotal scenes considered to be unacceptable.

Local clergy also objected to full-colour posters of blonde, bikini-clad starlets being displayed as come-hither point-of-sale advertising. Therefore, in the interest of public decency, many proprietors took to painting one-piece swimsuits over the bikinis with broad strokes and raising the neckline, which only served as a coded message that this picture was more risqué than normal.

During the glory days of film censorship, a belief grew up among small boys in Dublin that individual projectionists in local cinemas were cutting out the good parts and discarding them. Hence, a ritual root would take place through the cinema's bins for trophy outtakes, of which none were ever found.

Some films that were banned or cut were: *Animal Crackers*, *Brief Encounter*, *Cat on a Hot Tin Roof*, *The Graduate*, *High Society*, *I'm Alright Jack*, *Jailhouse Rock*, *The King of Kings*, *Little Big Man*, *On the Waterfront*, *The Quiet Man*, *Singin' in the Rain*, *The Texas Chainsaw Massacre* and *Ulysses*.

Quentin Tarrentino's *Natural Born Killers* (1994), starring Woody Harrelson and Juliette Lewis, was banned as being a danger to the mind of a nascent serial killer. However, film societies were allowed to show the film to its members; presumably on the premise that a serial killer would not be joining a film appreciation society and would, therefore, miss the instructional aspect of the movie.

BORN TO BE A ST KEVIN

If you're going to be a saint it is good to have saints about when you are born to guide you on the right path.

St Kevin is said to have been born at the Fort of the White Fountain in Leinster and to have been of royal descent. Legend has it that when he was born, an angel appeared and said he should be called Kevin, since nobody else was called that before him. Kevin, or Caomhain in Irish, means He of Blessed Birth, so there must have been some reason for such a name. As an infant he was baptised by St Cronan and was educated by St Petroc in Cornwall, where he was sent to study by his parents. However, the youngster was said to have a cross temper, which might also have been why he was sent away from home.

Unsurprisingly, when he grew to maturity he was ordained and then became a hermit at the Valley of the Two Lakes in Glendalough in County Wicklow (some said he chose the hermit life because he was being pursued by an over zealous devotee named Kathleen). After seven years of talking to himself in a cave, he was persuaded to give up his solitary life and he founded a monastery for the disciples he had attracted at Glendalough. So numerous were his followers that Glendalough became a small city in the mountains, becoming an episcopal see of its own, but was incorporated with Dublin in 1216.

Extravagant miracles were attributed to Kevin, many of which to the modern ear sound like yarns told around a sparkling

fire on a dark damp winter's night in the mountains. One such miracle reports how a cow used to lick Kevin awake in his cave and return to the others to yield more milk than any other cow. However, since Kevin's bed lies at the foot of a cliff the same cow would have had to have been a rock-climbing cow to see to Kevin each morning.

Kevin was reputed to have been 120 years old at his death, which was very old even for that time. His feast day is 3 June and he is a patron saint of Dublin.

St Kevin's bed of rock is still to be seen, at the foot of the cliff, where it always was. But there is no sign of an abseiling cow, thereabouts.

HOW TO BE A SAINT

Dublin's Venerable Matt Talbot is on his way to sainthood. When his day dawns he will join St Kevin and St Lawrence O'Toole as Dublin saints.

Dubliner Matt was one of thirteen children who lived his final days on Rutland Street Upper. A reformed alcoholic, he mortified his flesh, lived an ascetic life and attended to his religious duties scrupulously. He died on Granby Lane on his way to early morning mass and his remains lie in a tomb in Our Lady of Lourdes Church on Sean McDermott Street, not far from where he worked and lived. His name is now synonymous with fighting addiction of all kinds. Indeed, there is a particular devotion to Talbot among North Americans involved in a ministry to achieve or maintain sobriety.

To become a saint, the Congregation for Cause of Saints must evaluate your life. At this stage, if they are impressed with you, you get to be called a Servant of God. If the panel approves, the Pope proclaims the candidate – who must have been dead for five years – as venerable, which means the person is a role model of Catholic virtues. After venerable comes beatification – you get to be called Blessed in front of your name. This allows a candidate to be honoured by a group or region. In order to beatify a candidate, it must be shown that the person is responsible for a posthumous miracle, and in order for the candidate to be considered a saint there must be proof of a second posthumous miracle (all alleged miracles must be submitted to the Vatican for verification. Straightforward enough). If there is, the person is canonised. Once you are a saint, you are recommended to the entire Catholic Church for veneration and requests for intercession. That's it. Simple.

PROCESSIONS

The Feast of Corpus Christi is a moveable feast. It depends on the date of Easter Sunday: Easter is set as the Sunday following the full moon that falls on or after the vernal (spring) equinox; Corpus Christi is celebrated on the Thursday after Trinity Sunday; Pentecost is seven weeks after Easter; Trinity Sunday is the first Sunday after Pentecost.

At one time, every parish in Dublin held a Corpus Christi procession, either on the day itself or on the following Sunday. Such processions were large gatherings that closed roads to motor traffic, such was the press of people participating. Nowadays, many processions are conducted on footpaths or on Church grounds, such as the Corpus Christi procession for the Dublin Archdiocese, which takes place in the grounds of Clonliffe College, the former Catholic diocesan seminary for Dublin.

Processions of the Host are followed by Benediction of the Holy Sacrament and First Holy Communion children play a central role in the procession as they walk in a group with the congregation. Worship includes the singing of hymns during the celebration. In more religious times, a typical procession was led by a cross bearer, flanked by altar servers, followed by girl guides, brownies, boy scouts and children from local schools, followed by members of the defence forces and religious orders in town and the general lay congregation. Ceremonies usually ended with the entire congregation singing Faith of Our Fathers as loudly as they could and in tune, if possible.

THE CATACOMBS

The perspective of distance changes many things. The Catacombs – basically cellars of Georgian buildings around the Fitzwilliam/ Merrion Square area, frequented by writers and artists and those seeking late-night drinks in the late 1940s – seemed bohemian and daring in reputation. Now, however, they appear to have been more of a whatever-you're-having-yourself sort of place that acted as an antidote for some young adults to the strict regimen imposed on Dublin by the Emergency of the Second World War and the iron rule of the Catholic Church.

The Catacombs operated from the basement of a house on Fitzwilliam Place in the centre of Dublin and were begun by Dickie Wyman, an Englishman who moved to Dublin following the death of his boyfriend during the Second World War. Wyman opened a basement club in the flat that he rented and made some money from returning empty glass beer bottles the next morning for the refundable deposit on the bottles.

Not surprisingly, the Catacombs attracted young aspiring writers including Brendan Behan, Patrick Kavanagh, and J.P. Donleavy, who wrote about the place and the goings-on in his novel *The Gingerman*. Published in 1955, the book was set in Dublin in post-war 1947, but was banned in Ireland and the United States for obscenity. Nowadays, it can be purchased and read anywhere you like. Most people that might have been recognised from the description are dead now and residing in their own private, bespoke catacomb.

The Catacombs are no longer in operation as such, though other basements in the area sporadically manifest themselves as nightclubs, where very expensive drinks are served until the small hours of the morning. Though there is no money refunded on presentation of empty bottles.

3

FOLKLORE AND CUSTOMS

TOOTHACHE

Toothache has always been with us. Poor diet and lack of funds to pay for expensive dental treatment meant many people in Dublin of long ago sported sets of teeth with several gaps to be seen where rotten teeth were extracted by the local dentist when the pain had become too much for the patient to bear.

It was not uncommon for people with rotting teeth contemplating matrimony to have them extracted before the big day. In some cases, an acceptable wedding gift was to bear the cost of extraction of all the teeth of the bride or groom for the big day. In the case of a rushed marriage, advice often offered was 'not to tie with your tongue what you can't open with your teeth'. This was in the pre-velcro days when black knots were often attacked with the teeth to loosen their bond and to make them fall apart.

In modern times, one suggested response to toothache was to hold four to six cloves between tooth and gum. Clove oil is dabbed around the base of the tooth and in the rotten cavity, where appropriate. Garlic is also recommended for relieving toothache: mix a little garlic with some rock salt, apply to the throbbing tooth and hope for the best. It might work. If nothing else, people will move away and not bother to ask if you have a toothache.

An earlier cure was to acquire some sulphur and saltpetre, which were then placed in the tooth, causing the tooth to rot and fall out. This was the only means of extraction known in nineteenth-century Dublin, according to local experts from the Jobstown area of County Dublin. Nowadays, few people lose their teeth through decay. They are more likely to lose teeth in a punch-up or accident, which can sometimes be put down to carelessness or misplaced optimism.

Another doubtful remedy for toothache was as follows: go to a graveyard, kneel upon any grave, say three Paters and three Hail Mary's for the soul of the dead person lying beneath you, whoever they might be, and they with no use for working teeth, any more. Take a handful of grass from the grave, chew it well, spitting out each bite, without swallowing. After this process, were you to live a 100 years, you would never again have an aching tooth, though your teeth would probably be green for a while afterwards.

HYPOTHERMIA

Hypothermia is never far away when your clothing does not meet the climactic conditions of a Dublin winter: rain falling, a chilling wind blowing and all the while the sun peeking through the clouds, mocking us all.

Nowadays, clothing protects most people from the dangers of hypothermia, but it was not always so. Very often outdoor clothing was whatever was at hand – good-wear, light coats being passed along to become outdoor work coats as time passed. Some people kept warm by heating small stones on an open fire and placing them in their outer pockets, where they could slip their gloveless hands in to warm them from time to time. Further back in time, wood was gathered for fires that were more devoted to cooking food than heating people. Avoiding hypothermia while waiting for the food to boil was an everyday life skill. In one cure for exposure on Dublin's mountains, two men were out hunting hares when one fainted from cold and fatigue. According to local legend, placing two dead hares on his chest and two on his back revived him.

Men who worked outdoors in harsh weather would return home with the mark of the day's buffeting on them, so some would slip newspapers or stiff brown paper inside their outer coat to protect their chest from the wind and cold. In some places, scalteen was used as a sure-fire remedy for freezing bodies, for it was said that scalteen would make a corpse walk and take a nearly dead person back from the gates of Hades to the world of liveliness and jocularity. To be most effective, scalteen should be taken red-hot. It is made from half a pint of whiskey, half a pound of butter and six eggs; some add strained beef broth according to taste. Those taking it in extremis are advised to swallow it down and go straight to bed while they are still able to do so, for scalteen has a mind of its own when it comes to rejuvenating the mortal man, hypothermia or no.

FOOD

Dan Costello of Meath Street, Dublin was the first shopkeeper to sell Indian meal during the Great Famine of the 1840s when the potato crop failed and many people from the hinterland moved to the city of Dublin for sustenance. Cheap Indian meal, which had arrived from the United States, saved some people from starving outright. Others benefited from emergency soup kitchens set up by relief organisations, a number of which were administered by Protestant interests, leading some supplicants to change their religion to that of the soup providers. They were ever afterwards known as 'soupers', a derogatory title still in use for anyone who reneges on their beliefs for personal, temporary gain.

Nevertheless, the Famine did not affect Dublin as badly as it did other parts of the country. In rural areas around the city many people were able to live a self-sustained life from smallholdings attached to their homes, such as Malachi Horan from Jobstown in County Dublin, who would have stirabout, sweet milk and wheaten bread. Cabbage was the chief vegetable, sometimes eaten with a little meat and potatoes, and on Sunday mornings they had a cup of tea. Horan said they did not like tea much, but spent the week thinking about it.

Later, it became common practice for councils to provide large gardens with houses for occupants to grow their own produce and keep hens. In some cases, well-built concrete pig stys were provided. The pigs would be fed on sliced turnips, vegetable stalks, scraps and skins until large enough to be sold in the livestock market at

Stoneybatter on the North Circular Road, where cattle, sheep and pigs were offered for sale.

Up to the end of the twentieth century many food sellers called directly to homes on a daily basis, offering a range of basic food items, from fresh eggs and vegetables direct from farms to cakes and unwrapped bread from the bakeries. Fresh fish was sold mainly on Wednesdays and Fridays, following Church instructions not to eat meat on those days, and the sellers also offered specialities of unpasteurised milk poured into the buyer's jug by the seller. Meals during this time generally consisted of a light breakfast, a full dinner in the middle of the day and a light supper known as 'tea' at the end of the working day.

CLOTHING

Early Dublin medieval dress was simple in style. Both men and women wore the same basic garments: an inner tunic and a topcoat or mantle topped with a hooded cloak.

Much later on, large coats called cotamores were worn. The cotamore was a frieze coat that reached to the ankles and which had attached to it a cape as far as the wrists. These coats were heavy but very warm – a first-rate protection when driving. Beneath the coat, the coat-wearer wore corduroy or moleskin breeches above grey stockings. Some outdoor workers often wore jute sack around their shoulders, held by a nail at the chest, as a rudimentary cape, although these would also double in weight when wet.

Members of religious orders wore their order's uniforms and as such were readily identified as members. Schoolchildren in well-to-do areas wore the uniform of their school. Poorer districts wore what they could find or afford. However, in a show of power, bishops wore sumptuous costumes at ceremonies. Pearls, diamonds, silks and precious embroidered capes were a great favourite among the humble men of religion.

Hats

When a man's cap is on, his roof is thatched, they say. And while today's Dubliner wears no hat as such – preferring to show off his sprouting hair or shiny baldness – he once wore a workaday hat or cap, and had a Sunday best as well.

A felt, half-tall hat, now seen among wild tourists around Temple Bar, but once worn in all sobriety by normal folk, was known as a nailer's chimney and a Bailen's hat was the hat of choice by coachmen, who had to sit out in the elements all day without shelter – the leaf of the hat was so wide that it gave cover to the shoulders. However, the hats were made of wool and weighed 6kg when dry and almost 13kg when wet.

Women wore scarves for everyday use and kept a hat for special occasions, much like today.

BRIGID DANCING AND THE WREN

Pagan times are not far below the surface in Dublin. A pastime celebrated in February, in Brittas, was the Bride Oge in honour of St Bridget, or the pagan goddess Bridget, depending on who was telling the story.

During the celebrations, a little figure made of straw and bits of coloured cloth and with hair made from sheep's wool was carried on a pole – this was the Bride Oge, or young Bridget. The men who carried it dressed up in long, white shirts and made beards and moustaches for their faces and woolly wigs for their heads so that they could go in procession in disguise (at a time when there were plenty of sheep about – catching their coats in briars as they passed by – there was plenty of free wool to be had on the roadside for face decoration). They went from door to door, where householders gave them some money. At neighbours' houses they said a prayer, sang and danced to the music of fiddles and goatskin tambourines.

Once summer came along, dancing on Sundays would begin. Someone would be made auctioneer and he would hold a tin plate in his hand, into which a person tossed a bid for a tune: perhaps for oneself, perhaps to please a partner, or, attract a fancy.

The Wren Boys made a similar rush of things on St Stephen's Day, the day after Christmas Day. Long ago, they got given a threepenny or a sixpenny piece at most houses, so that by the end of the day they had enough money to pay for a hooley that night. On 26 December, the body of a small bird was paraded from house to house in a small, decorated box, where money was requested to bury the Wren. In return, the household was entertained with music and a song before the Wren Boys moved on to the next house. The song began as follows:

The wren oh the wren he's the king of all birds,
On St Stephen's day he got caught in the furze,
So it's up with the kettle and it's down with the pan
Won't you give me a penny for to bury the wren?

HIRING FAIR

Dublin City and county once had a rural hinterland that had the name of being Dublin, but was more associated with country ways than city ways. The hiring fair for male farm workers was one such country tradition that took place on Tallaght's main street, many years ago.

On 15 August each year, farmers met and struck a rate for wages for the year. It would be about half-a-crown a day in the late nineteenth century, good enough money for the time (there were eight half crowns in a pound, which was worth €1.27 in modern value). If a man was to be housed and fed, then the rate shrank to a shilling a day, of which there were twenty in a pound. However, farm workers were not always fully welcomed as members of the farmer's entourage, with some farmers equating them to farm livestock and offering shelter to them in farm outbuildings and sheds.

Available workers would walk in from neighbouring towns seeking to be taken on. Once they reached the main street, they would stand at an old forge on the street to show they were interested in being hired, although some cute farmers stood out the road and engaged the best and strongest of the workers on the way into the town, forsaking all others. Those who stood at the forge would stick a small clay pipe in the band of the hat as a signal of availability. When hired, the pipe would be removed from the hat and put safely in the pocket. No pipe displayed meant he was not available for hire.

Some of these strong, able-bodied lads could reap an acre a day on their own, using very basic hand tools. Each man carried a sharpening whetstone in a pouch on his belt for sharpening his tools as he went through his day. Tallaght's main street would be full with farmers looking for the best workers and men anxious to be hired. Once bargains were struck and deals made, laughing and storytelling took over. Some would dance, sing, joke or wrestle another to see who was best at it. Such a congregation attracted travelling ballad-singers and fiddlers, who entertained for whatever recompense was available to them from the gathered men and hiring farmers.

MARRIAGE

Where once Dublin marriages took place in churches, couples can now marry in many other places, including Dublin Zoo.

There are two sets of registrars to choose from: one for Roman Catholic marriages and another for Protestant and civil marriages. Three months' written notice of the parties' intention to wed must be given to the registrar for the district in which they wish to be married. No quickies allowed.

Wedding matches were often made by the families and a dowry was given by the bride's father of money or stock. He also paid for the wedding breakfast. A usual time for weddings was on Mondays or Saturdays, although an unlucky date to be married was the 13th of a month and May was considered an unlucky month in which to wed.

When a newly married couple told their twentieth-century Dublin wedding guests they were touring Ireland for their honeymoon, it actually meant they were going to an auntie's house down the country for a week or less, depending on funds and the auntie. Newly-weds who could not afford to honeymoon somewhere else were supposed to stay indoors for a week, perhaps in the hope that people would think they were away somewhere if they were not seen in their usual haunts. Custom also dictated that a sharp knife should not be used in preparation of food for that week. In a time before pre-wrapped and prepared food was freely available, this might result in near starvation and a severe trying of matrimonial bonds if the two people did not meet one another halfway.

Marriage was for life, until divorce was introduced into Ireland by the passing of divorce legislation in 1997.

WAKES AND BURIALS

The Irish wake harks back to pagan times and for that reason clergy of all beliefs were generally against them, preferring to control the obsequies themselves in the surety of their churches. Or, they may just have been against the shenanigans that could ensue when steady drinking, singing and storytelling went on in the wake house.

In modern Dublin, funeral homes have taken over much of the preparation for ushering the dead's remains out of this world. In the old days, however, when someone died they were waked in their own home before being brought to the church for the funeral prayers and mass; sometimes they went directly from the wake house to the graveyard and the newly dug grave.

The traditional Irish wake took place while a body was in the wake house – generally the house where they had lived during their latter years. The corpse would usually be displayed in an open coffin in the parlour or living room of the house, whichever was considered the best room, and friends and neighbours would come to say farewell.

While there was keening involved from time to time – and some say the cadence of the experienced keener is identical to the call of the banshee, who calls the living to death – the wake was more a celebration of life than a lament. Copious amounts of food and drink were provided and consumed by the mourners, who did their best to keep each other's spirits up by telling stories, anecdotes and amusing memories of the recently deceased who was laid out before them.

In latter times, a person died and was brought to their home for waking. Close friends and relatives would keep watch at the coffin through the night, sometimes in relays, and prayers would be said. Visitors, on arrival, would bless themselves with holy water and sprinkle a drop on the corpse in silent prayer.

The wake took place in the period of time from death until the body was brought to the care of the church, which was generally the evening before the day of burial, a ceremony known as the Removal. The following morning, a Church service, or mass, was

held, with music and song and spoken farewell. The coffin was then conveyed to the graveyard, where final prayers were said before burial.

BANSHEE AND HEADLESS COACHMEN

If you hear the banshee calling it is usually a sign that someone is about to die, for the Bean Sí is a fairy woman who has foreseen death and comes to warn of death's impending arrival. It is said, by some, that the banshee wails for some special families who are believed to have banshees attached to them. Chosen families are said to be those with an Ó or Mac prefix to their family name: Ó is generally given to old Celtic families and Mac is associated with later arrivals, invaders if you like, who came later to Ireland.

Ó means 'of', 'O'Connor' then being 'of Connor', who started the family off some time ago in the mists of long-forgotten memory. Mac means 'the son of', which includes daughters as well, just to include everyone and upset nobody. However, since most Irish names expressed in the Irish language begin with an Ó or Mac, it seems that nearly everyone alive and of an Irish family is entitled to a scream from a banshee when death hastens down the road, seeking the house of the next to die.

Another portent of death was the cóiste bodhar (the deaf or silent coach, a death coach). What was more, the driver was also headless. It was said that in parts of Dublin, and Ringsend in particular, a phantom coach drawn by black horses would come galloping along the street when someone died. It would stop outside the wake house and take away any living soul unfortunate enough to be standing there. Unsurprisingly, few stayed around to see what might happen. But, tradition had it that once such a coach arrived it would not return empty.

Of course, unbelievers say there was no such coach. It was a myth. It was a story circulated by the sack-'em-ups, or grave robbers, to keep people inside the house, where the curtains were already closed out of respect for the recently deceased and where mirrors were turned to the wall, for fear of attracting the devil's likeness reflected in the mirror. Closed curtains and empty streets helped grave robbers to pass along unseen, with fresh bodies stolen from any cemetery that had seen a recent interment. They would then sell them to a waiting medical establishment for dissection, in the interests of eighteenth-century medical research.

ST PATRICK'S DAY

St Patrick's Day or the Feast of St Patrick, known in Irish as Lá Fhéile Pádraig, is a cultural and religious holiday celebrated by the Irish and those who aspire to be Irish, if only for a day. The day is known colloquially as St Paddy's Day, Paddy being a diminutive of Patrick, although some Americans argue that it is called St Patty's Day, but Patty is a woman's name, so that can't be correct – St Patrick had a beard, so he was a man, and therefore a Paddy.

The day is named after St Patrick (*c.* AD 385–461), who is credited with bringing the Christian faith to Ireland; a land where he had been enslaved as a boy before escaping and taking holy orders and becoming an evangelising bishop. When in full flight, he explained to pagans the mystery of there being three divine persons in one God. He showed them that the shamrock has three leaves in one, and that it was much the same with God. This satisfied them and they converted in droves to the new religion. Consequently, Irish people wear a shamrock on St Patrick's Day to show they understand this and will always remember the lesson taught to them by St Patrick.

St Patrick's Day is a public holiday in Ireland, Newfoundland, Labrador and Montserrat, and, in some countries, local authorities are persuaded to dye their waters green for the day. The day is widely celebrated by the Irish diaspora, generally on the day or at weekends contiguous to 17 March, and the Irish Taoiseach visits the American President each year in the White House to present a bowl of shamrock to the American people as a friendly gesture between great powers. Indeed, so highly do rotating Irish governments rate the day that most government ministers fly off out of the country to celebrate the day and 'Irishness' with other public representatives in other countries. Most people, if asked, would admit to not missing the politicians at all once the party gets going.

The main parade takes place in Dublin, where people have enjoyed the thing so much they have re-named it St Patrick's Festival, and now make a week or so out of it. Celebrations generally involve public parades that parade anywhere they may, or, may not, festivals (céilithe) and the wearing of green gear or shamrocks, or both. Strange hats and false beards are worn, but nobody pretends they know they are not real, so everyone is happy, more or less.

4

STRANGE
BUT TRUE

Matt Talbot lived and died among the Dublin poor. When he was
dead people began to pray to him for intercession in their own lives,
with particular emphasis on addiction.

Talbot was born into poverty as the son of an alcoholic father,
becoming an alcoholic in his own right, before giving it all up
at 28 years old and turning to a different form of obsession –
religious observance.

He started school late, at 11 years of age, and attended nearby
O'Connell's School so sporadically that he was listed as a truant in
the school roll. Yet, in later life he took to reading and studying the
lives of the early Irish monks. He lived the life of an ascetic amid the
busy life of a city, while continuing with his work as a labourer in a
dockside timber yard. He attended mass daily each morning before
work, as well as attending on a Sunday. Indeed, it was not unusual
to find Talbot kneeling on the steps of a church while awaiting the
opening of its doors for early morning mass attendance. Before
arriving at the church, he rose through the night to kneel in prayer in
his own home.

Talbot fell dead, in 1925, at 69 years of age, on his way into
church on a Sunday. When his body was examined, it was found
that beneath his clothing he wore chains wrapped about him so as
to mortify his body. It was also rumoured that he had slept beneath
a single blanket on a single plank of wood, with another block of
wood for a pillow, in emulation of earlier ascetics.

Talbot never married. In his ageing years he had lived with his
mother in 19 Rutland Street, Upper, who predeceased him. In the
national census of 1911, it was recorded that six families shared this
three-story-over-basement house.

Talbot's coffined remains may be visited in his parish church on Sean McDermott Street in a purpose-built shrine made of Wicklow granite.

ST MICHAN'S MUMMIES

There was once only one bridge across the Liffey in Dublin city. It catered for travellers on a great road that ran down through the country, passing Dublin on its way – an early, rudimentary motorway, of sorts. The main road from Tara in County Meath to Wicklow and the southern counties crossed the Liffey at this point. Its descendant spans the river at the Four Courts from Upper Bridge Street on the south to Church Street on the other side.

On Church Street, surprisingly enough, stands St Michan's church. Intriguingly, underneath the church lie five burial vaults containing the mummified remains of members of some of Dublin's most influential families from the seventeenth, eighteenth and nineteenth centuries. One of the vaults includes the remains of the Shears brothers, the 1798 revolutionaries, while in another there is the remains of the 'Crusader' – a man who has been dead for 650 years, which is a long time to be lying about in a vault, going nowhere. In another coffin resides the body of a man with his feet cut off, a punishment perhaps, or a rudimentary response by a coffiner to a man too tall to fit in his own casket. There is also a nun lying in one and a lay woman in another.

A constant dry atmosphere has caused the mummification of the bodies and preservation of coffins in the vaults, although the coffins have now cracked open and the casket lids are off, exposing bodies partly covered with taut, leathery skin and coated in a thick layer of dust. They are gone but still with us. Spookily enough, it is said that Dubliner Bram Stoker, creator of the never-out-of-print *Dracula* (1897), is believed to have visited the vaults in the company of his family.

The present building dates from about 1685, when it was rebuilt. Not only that, but the St Michan's organ is said to be one of the oldest in the country and is still in use. It is believed that George F. Handel played it when composing *The Messiah* in 1741, which received its world premiere across the river in what is now Fishamble Street on the extremity of modern-day Temple Bar.

ANYBODY THERE?

A Dublin couple accepted damages in a court case after council officials accidentally boarded them up inside their home. Tristan Ua Ceithearnaigh, 46, and his partner, Elisa Udtohan, 25, were awarded €76,000 after a court heard that, in December 2010, workers began boarding up their home on Eugene Street, Dublin with corrugated iron sheets over the front door and windows as the couple sat at home with their four-month-old baby daughter, Mia.

On the day of the incident, the couple ignored a ring on the doorbell, as they were not expecting anyone to call, but matters took a turn for the worse when the noise of activity outside increased: someone was hammering at the door. They believed they were under siege, and, as they watched, six-inch fixing nails came through the doorframe, blocking out all the light.

Hearing voices within, those outside asked the besieged couple if they were squatters, but were told the property was a privately rented house and they certainly were not there under any guise whatsoever, other than that of people who had a right to be there. After some conversation, someone in authority outside called a halt to the hammering and workers started pulling the large nails out of the doorframe, removing the sheets of corrugated iron as they went. As the bewildered residents looked on, workmen then began fixing the corrugated iron sheets they had removed from the couple's home to a vacant house next door.

The couple claimed they had to be treated for emotional distress and left the house shortly after the incident.

In court, Dublin City Council denied falsely imprisoning the couple or defaming them by creating the impression they were squatters or being evicted. However, the court agreed with the couple and awarded them substantial damages.

MRS HITLER

Adolf Hitler's sister-in-law grew up in Clondalkin in County Dublin. Bridget Elizabeth Hitler, *née* Dowling, married Alois Hitler Jr, Adolf's older half-brother, in 1910. She was subsequently to be the mother of Alois Hitler's son: William Patrick Hitler.

Not to be outdone in family fantasy, Alois Hitler Jr claimed to be a wealthy hotelier touring Europe (in actual fact he was a waiter in Dublin's Shelbourne Hotel) when, in 1909, the suave gent met Bridget and her father, William, for the first time at the Dublin Horse Show. The following June, the 17-year-old Bridget eloped to London to marry Alois. In time, they moved with William Patrick, their son, to Liverpool.

All was far from serene in the Hitler household, for, according to Bridget, Alois become violent and started to beat their son. When Alois returned to Germany in 1914 to establish himself in business, Bridget refused to go with him, so he decided to abandon Bridget and their son in Britain. Once home, however, the First World War interrupted Alois' career path. Alois married once more, bigamously, and sent word after the war to Bridget, through a third party, that he was dead. However, that ruse fell through and in 1924 he was charged with bigamy in Germany.

As Adolf rose to power through his Nazi party and war loomed in 1939, Bridget joined her son on a tour of the United States, where he was to lecture on his uncle, Adolf. Mother and son settled in the United States, leaving their home in Britain behind them.

Bridget later wrote a book – which she herself described as fanciful – in which Adolf came to stay with his brother and Bridget in Britain in 1913 to avoid conscription at home and she advised him to trim the ends off his moustache. She also claimed to have introduced Adolf to astrology. None of these claims were ever verified.

After the war, Bridget and her son Patrick Hitler settled on Long Island under the pseudonym of Stuart-Houston. Alois Hitler Jr died in 1956 in Hamburg, Germany. Bridget died in November 1969 in the United States and Patrick Hitler died suddenly in 1987. He is buried with his mother in Holy Sepulchre Cemetery in Coram, Long Island.

DUBLIN WOMAN SHOOTS MUSSOLINI

Italian fascist leader Benito Mussolini almost died at the hands of a Dublin woman, who shot him in the face, long before he committed his country to war in 1939.

On 7 April 1926 in Rome, Mussolini had just given a speech to the International Congress of Surgeons, and, while a band started to play *Giovinezza*, the National Fascist Party's official anthem, Violet Gibson fired three shots at him, with the intention of ending his life. Mussolini snapped his head to attention on hearing the ditty and the bullets flew through the space lately occupied by his head.

Although the 50-year-old Gibson had fired the revolver at nearly point-blank range, she failed to kill Mussolini, much to her bemusement. A bullet did, however, pass through Mussolini's nose, leaving burn marks on exit. Nonetheless, within minutes of the shooting, Mussolini reappeared, wearing a large bandage over his nose, probably with a slight headache to boot.

The unsuccessful Gibson was grabbed by the crowd, who were intent on taking her life in response to her attack, but police officers rescued her from the mob and arrested her for questioning. Although Dublin born, she was deported to Britain on Mussolini's orders, where she spent her remaining thirty years in a Northampton mental asylum. She died in 1956 at the age of 80.

Gibson was daughter to Edward Gibson, Lord Chancellor of Ireland (who became Lord Ashbourne in 1886). She grew up in comfort and privilege between Dublin and London. In 1906, Gibson made her first trip to Rome, after which she began to read the lives of the saints and was absorbed by their teachings. She began to idolise Italy as the land of Dante, Fra Angelico and St Francis and became a peace activist in the lead-up to the First World War.

Violet was acutely aware of the dangers posed by Mussolini and took it upon herself to eliminate him, without success, forgoing her own freedom for the rest of her life in the attempt. Bizarrely Lucia

Joyce, the only daughter of James Joyce, and at one time the lover of Samuel Beckett, spent her last thirty years in Northampton's St Andrew's hospital for mental diseases, also rarely meeting anyone from the outside world.

CHURCHILL

Winston Churchill, the British Second World War leader, lived in Dublin as a small boy. When Winston's grandfather, John Winston Spencer-Churchill, the Duke of Marlborough, was appointed Viceroy to Ireland in 1876, his son, Lord Randolph Churchill, arrived in Dublin as his Private Secretary, bringing his young son, Winston Churchill, with him.

Lord Randolph lived with his family in the Private Secretary's Lodge and Winston roamed the Viceregal gardens, reportedly driving happily along the wide paths on a donkey and cart. Winston later recalled witnessing his grandfather talking loudly to a crowd gathered for the unveiling of the Lord Gough equestrian statue in 1878, in Phoenix Park. The statue of Lord Gough, the great warrior of India, the conqueror of the Punjab, was intended for a city location – the west side of O'Connell Bridge – but Dublin Corporation refused the request to place it there, and so it was landed in Phoenix Park.

In the second half of the twentieth century, having survived the dropping of a bomb at the nearby Dog Pond by a German aircraft in 1942, the Gough statue was attacked with explosives by nationalists set on removing all vestiges of British rule.

On 23 July 1957 it was removed by park management and sold. An earlier attack had seen the statue's head being removed and dumped into the River Liffey, from where it was recovered, and replaced.

However, this was not to be the end of Lord Gough's ride. In 2010, Misneach, an equestrian feature, was unveiled as publicly funded art in Dublin's Ballymun, a few miles away. It featured a reproduction of Gough's horse. Artist John Byrne constructed the mould for the horse from the Gough memorial at Chillingham Castle in Northumberland, where the statue was re-erected and restored after its removal from Dublin. The new work featured a moulding of local girl Tony Marie Shields as the rider. The moulds of girl and horse were combined to create the new piece, which stands on Main Street Ballymun as part of its regeneration project, a long way from the Punjab.

OUZEL GALLEY RETURNS FROM SEA

The Central Bank on Dublin's Dame Street hides a memory of a lost ship, the *Ouzel Galley*, that returned to Dublin after many years at sea, when all hope had been given up of seeing her or her crew again. Indeed, some of the crews' wives had even remarried, on the assumption that their earlier husbands had departed this life somewhere at sea. Many started new families with new fathers, so there was great confusion when the lads arrived home for tea.

The *Ouzel Galley* set sail from Ringsend, Dublin in 1695 en-route to Smyrna in the Ottoman Empire, now Izmir in Turkey, on a trade mission on behalf of Ferris, Twigg & Cash of Dublin. Her captain, Eoghan Massey of Waterford, and his crew were scheduled to return the following year, having engaged in trade. But, three years later, in 1698, when there had been no word of the ship, a panel of Dublin merchants ruled the ship had been lost with her crew of forty on board and that compensation should be paid out to the owners and insurers of the ship. However, after a further two years, in 1700, the ship sailed up the River Liffey, to the bewilderment of Dubliners watching from the quayside.

Captain Massey said his men had spent five years in captivity at the hands of Algerian corsairs, who had used the ship to engage in acts of piracy. The returned ship was loaded down with booty on its return to its home port.

Rumours and allegations soon spread around the city. It was claimed Massey and his men had engaged in piracy and the

contentious matter of an insurance payout for a ship not lost but now returned was raised.

Ownership of the cargo was hotly debated: the owners claimed it as theirs, the insurers said they now owned whatever was of value, and the crew felt that since they had fought over it and brought it home they should have an interest in the spoils. Solomon-like, a panel of merchants decided that all monies remaining following compensation of owners and insurers should go towards a fund for the alleviation of poverty among Dublin's decayed merchants.

An Ouzel Galley Society was instituted to determine commercial differences, by arbitration. They met at Commercial Buildings, where the Central Bank building now stands. Originally, the building incorporated a pedestrian walkway to Crown Alley through its internal courtyard. The current Central Bank plaza was an entry and passageway through the old building.

In the twentieth century, it was planned to rotate the original building some 90 degrees to allow for the Central Bank to be built, and then to rebuild the original façade on Dame Street. The stonework was dismantled and numbered for reinstallation, but it didn't happen. Instead, a facsimile was erected to the side in its place after the original was demolished to make way for the Central Bank development.

NOW YOU SEE IT, NOW YOU SEE MORE OF IT: IRA RAID ON MAGAZINE

Dublin's Phoenix Park now lies within the city limits; its front gate is at Parkgate Street in the City Council area. But when Sir Edward Fisher built his country residence in 1611, on the hill that gave its name to Phoenix Park, little did he think that a powder magazine would one day be built on the ruins of his house.

That same magazine, in 1939, became the scene of a Christmas escapade that takes some believing. The European War had begun in September and nationalists' eyes were turned northwards, where six Irish counties still lay within the United Kingdom. The Army of the Irish Free Sate was by then holding munitions in the magazine, and before the raid began IRA lookouts were posted at the Islandbridge Gates to the historic Park, within which the magazine now lies.

On 23 December 1939 the fort was raided for arms by the illegal Irish Republican Army – the military wing of those who had refused to recognise the treaty of 1922 and the consequent Irish Free State. A convoy of forty lorries was brought in to remove ammunition, rifles and machine-guns. The raiders then departed into the night with their haul. Two IRA men were arrested in the park at the time of the raid.

However, such was the swift response from the Defence Forces to the theft of their stored weapons that all Christmas leave was cancelled and searching began for the armaments. Just five days later, on 28 December, most of the stolen equipment had been recovered by the army, mainly from dumps in the midlands. It wasn't until the recovery operation was over that they realised more weaponry than was stolen in the magazine raid had been recovered, such was the diligence of the search and the determination of the searchers to recover their lost materials.

5

SPORTS AND GAMES

GAELIC

Michael Cusack and a group of men formed the Dublin Hurling Club in 1882. Two years later, Cusack helped found the Gaelic Athletic Association (GAA) in Thurles, County Tipperary on 1 November 1884. Before that, however, the Dubs needed somewhere to play – always a good idea for a team game. With no designated space for the club in Phoenix Park, where they wished to play, the All-Ireland Polo Club agreed to the use of their pitch on the Nine Acres by the new hurlers.

The first planned hurling match had to be postponed because no manufacturer in Dublin knew how to make hurleys or sliotars (balls) for the game, since the skills had fallen into disuse when no matches were played. When they were finally produced some time later, away they went each weekend on the grass near the Wellington Monument. In the early games, organisers allowed spectators to join in and, consequently, many people chased a sliotar around Phoenix Park, to the enjoyment and consternation of all, as battle waxed and waned. As a result, Regulation 25 of the 1919 Phoenix Park Regulations includes an admonition to park constables to prevent ball games being played near the monument.

The club eventually collapsed, but the GAA prospered, purchasing its current headquarters and stadium in Dublin in 1913. Alterations and modifications have continued through the years ever since. In 1961, a record 90,556 spectators attended the All-Ireland Football Final between Down (3-6) and Offaly (2-8).

In February 2007, Croke Park hosted its first match under floodlights when Dublin (0-10) played Tyrone (0-11) in the opening match of the

National Football League. The floodlights give the power of 2,000 candles to the playing surface, though playing under floodlights seems a more hazardous engagement than playing by a more gentle candlelight.

Croke Park has also hosted a number of other major events:

1972: the bout between Muhammad Ali and Al 'Blue' Lewis, in which Ali was victorious.

1984: a concert by Neil Diamond – the first artist to perform at the Park.

1985: the first of U2's many Croke Park concerts.

2003: Nelson Mandela, U2, The Corrs and Muhammad Ali were among the 80,000 spectators who attended the opening of the Special Olympic Games.

2007: Ireland and France became the first rugby teams and Wales and Ireland became the first soccer teams to play in the stadium.

2011: Queen Elizabeth II and the Duke of Edinburgh visited Croke Park on 18 May as part of their State visit to Ireland, though they did not kick a ball about on the pitch.

2012: the stadium hosted the closing ceremony of the 50th International Eucharistic Congress, with some 80,000 people in attendance.

DUBLIN OLYMPIANS

Dublin has had its share of Olympians, from runners to boxers and even a poet.

Oliver St John Gogarty, poet
Art competitions at the Olympic Games were held from 1912 to 1948 and in 1924, Gogarty won a bronze medal in France in the Paris Mixed Literature section for his poem *Ode pour les Jeux de Tailteann*. He is the only Irish poet to win an Olympic medal for poetry.

Ronnie Delany, runner
Delany, who specialised in middle-distance running, won a gold medal by finishing first in the 1500m event at the 1956 Summer Olympics in Melbourne. He then won a bronze medal in the 1500m at the 1958 European Athletics Championships in Stockholm, Sweden.

Fred Tiedt, boxer

Tiedt won a silver medal at the 1956 Summer Olympics in Melbourne, Australia in the welterweight division – he just missed gold by losing a split decision to Nicolae Linca of Romania. In 1957, he won a bronze medal at the European Amateur Boxing Championships in Prague.

David Wilkins, sailor

Wilkins competed at five Olympics between 1972 and 1992, winning silver in 1980 with partner James Wilkinson at the Moscow Olympics in the Flying Dutchman class.

Michael Carruth, boxer

Michael Carruth, the southpaw boxer from Dublin, won a welterweight gold medal at the 1992 Summer Olympics in Barcelona, in 2006.

Michelle Smith de Bruin, swimmer

Smith de Bruin became Ireland's most successful Olympian to date when, in the 1996 Summer Olympics in Atlanta, she was a triple gold medallist at the Atlanta Games for the 400m individual medley, 400m freestyle and 200m individual medley. She also won the bronze medal for the 200m butterfly event.

Kenny Egan, boxer

Egan won a silver medal in the 81kg light-heavyweight boxing final at the 2008 Olympics in Beijing, China. He won the European gold medal in the 2008 Athens Olympic Qualifiers and a European bronze medal in 2006 and 2010 at light-heavyweight.

Cián O'Connor, equestrian

O'Connor won a bronze medal at the London Olympic games in 2012. In the 2004 Summer Olympics in Athens he won the gold medal in individual jumping, but later lost his medal after the sports ruling body found his horse had banned substances in its system during the games. However, the FEI said it was satisfied that O'Connor was not involved in a deliberate attempt to influence the performance of the horse.

RUNNERS

The Dublin Marathon is an annual event normally held on the last Monday in October, which is a public holiday in Ireland. Begun in 1980, the early marathons were made up of a great many Irish entrants, but by 2007 half of the 11,000 race participants were from overseas. In 2009 a record was set when some 12,799 runners started the event, with 10,446 finishing the course.

Beginning on Fitzwilliam Square in the city centre, the course travels around the north and the south sides of Dublin before concluding at Merrion Square, not far from the starting point. The course is generally flat, with the exception of long, uphill drags through Phoenix Park.

The Dublin Marathon was founded by a group of enthusiasts led by Noel Carroll. Carroll was a middle-distance runner who competed at the 1964 Olympic Games in Tokyo in the Men's 800m, and then at the 1968 Olympics in Mexico City in the 400m and 800m. In the inaugural race in 1980 some 2,100 participants took part, with as many again lining the streets in excitement to encourage the runners. Some 1,420 finished the course. Dick Hooper of Raheny Shamrock Athletic Club was first home in a time of 2 hours 16 minutes and 14 seconds. The women's winner was Carey May, who finished in 2 hours 42 minutes and 11 seconds. May also won the Osaka Ladies Marathon in 1983 and 1985.

In 1995, a Kilkenny man created heated controversy when he joined the leading runners for the final 3 miles and finished with the leaders in 7th home position. Leading runners claimed he joined the race as it left Phoenix Park for the home stretch. He finished in an alleged time of 2 hours 25 minutes. Afterwards, in an agreed statement with the organisers, the impostor admitted he did not complete the full marathon distance and he was withdrawn from the results. He had to return his finisher's plaque, leaving him with nothing to show for running 3 miles.

In 2001, the marathon became part of the Dublin Race Series. It now includes pre-marathon events of 5 miles, 10 kilometres, 10 miles and half marathon distance over the preceding months, run in Phoenix Park and Swords.

RUGBY

Lansdowne Football Club is one of the oldest rugby clubs in Ireland. Its pitch is also the oldest international rugby ground in the world. Founded in 1872 by Henry W.D. Dunlop as the Irish Champion Athletic Club, the club's home ground is on Lansdowne Road, which doubles as the Irish international stadium where international soccer matches are held. The stadium was named after the nearby road, which was named after William Petty-FitzMaurice, First Marquess of Lansdowne. Not content with being a Marquis, William was also the Earl of Shelbourne, and Shelbourne Road is also named after him, though where he had his post delivered is now lost to time.

Dunlop, in conjunction with Edward Dillon, took a 69-year lease from the Pembroke Estate, paying a ground rent of £60 per annum. They began with a cinder running path of a quarter-mile and laid down the Lansdowne Tennis Club ground. While he was at it, Dunlop also started a Lansdowne archery club, a Lansdowne cricket club and the Lansdowne Rugby Football Club.

The first representative rugby match at the venue was an inter-provincial fixture between Leinster and Ulster in December 1876. On 11 March 1878, Lansdowne Road hosted its first international rugby fixture against England, making it the world's oldest rugby union Test venue. The first international soccer match took place in 1900 between Ireland (0) and England (2) on Saint Patrick's Day.

On 20 November 1988, Boston College beat Army 38–24 in the Emerald Isle Classic, the first major NCAA American football game ever played in Europe. It was played in front of 42,525 fans. At the time, it was officially estimated that the game brought some US$30 million in spending to the local economy, a lot of money for one game.

From 1990 to 2006, the ground was used for the vast majority of home fixtures by the Republic of Ireland soccer team by the Football Association of Ireland, which leased the ground for international soccer matches.

On 15 February 1995, English football hooligans caused the referee to abandon the game between England and the Republic sides after just 27 minutes, when the visiting fans engaged in an organised riot.

The grounds have also hosted sell-out concerts by Michael Jackson, U2 and Robbie Williams, among others.

In 2007, the old stadium was demolished to make way for the construction of the present-day Aviva Stadium, a 50,000 all-seater soccer and rugby stadium that opened in 2010.

FORE SAID CAPTAIN BLIGH

Captain William Bligh of the *Bounty* had a hand in the formation of the Royal Dublin Golf Club, founded in 1885, as a private members' club. It is Ireland's second oldest golf club. Before this venture, Bligh had survived being set adrift after the mutiny of his crew on HMS *Bounty* in 1789. He arrived in Dublin in 1800 on a new posting and was invited to make suggestions on providing shipping with a safe, straight and deep approach into Dublin City. Consequently, the Bull Wall, a 3km breakwater extending out from Dollymount, was built on Bligh's recommendations. Subsequent silting outside the wall saw a sandbank develop into an island (Bull Island), which produced an ideal base for the greens and fairways of the Royal Dublin Golf Club.

The club, an 18-hole links course, shares the island with a flat 5km beach within Dublin Bay, much enjoyed by Dubliners. Designed originally by Harry Colt, the links was extended under the guidance of golf architect Martin Hawtree. The club, then known just as the Dublin Golf Club, was initially located near the Hibernian Military School in Phoenix Park before moving to Sutton. Five years later, in 1889, it moved to its present home, by then having become Royal. The links now covers 65 hectares. The Royal Dublin held the Irish Open three times – in 1983, 1984 and 1985.

Bull Island is connected to the island by a causeway and by an atmospheric single-traffic-only wooden road bridge. The bridge was installed in 1819 to facilitate the construction of the stonewall and has been in clattering use ever since. Many Dubliners learned to drive on the firm, flat sandy foreshore at low tide. However, motor access is now limited to a portion of the island near the Bull Bridge and two sections reached from the causeway at Raheny.

Bull Island was declared a Bird Sanctuary in the 1930s, a UNESCO Biosphere Reserve in 1981, a Nature Reserve in 1988 and a Wetland of International Importance under the Ramsar Convention on 6 September 1988. It also qualifies for designation as a Nature Heritage Area, Special Protection Area, and Special Area of Conservation and was declared a Special Amenity Area in 1994.

Apart from wandering golfers seeking lost balls, the island is home, at various times, to 8,000 wild fowl and 26,000 waders, with up to 180 different bird species being recorded. More than 300 species of plants have also been recorded, including some rare and officially protected species.

And not a single mutineer to be seen.

THE LONG ARM OF A BOXER AND THE HYPNOTIST

Dan Donnelly was a pioneer of professional boxing and the first Irish-born heavyweight champion. He was born on Townsend Street in Dublin's dockland.

Donnelly would go to great lengths to avoid street fighting, but, in a good cause, he was known to be handy with his fists and he became a local fighting hero.

When prize fights were introduced, Donnelly fought at the Curragh in County Kildare in September 1814 in Belcher's Hollow, later renamed Donnelly's Hollow, for obvious reasons. By the time the bout was to start, an estimated 20,000 people stood on the sides of the hollow. Donnelly defeated Tom Hall on that date and in a bout the following year he defeated the English boxer George Cooper, to wild acclaim.

A destitute Donnelly died at 32 years of age on 18 February 1820 and was buried in Bully's Acre at Kilmainham. But, grave robbers took and delivered his corpse to a Dr Hall, an eminent surgeon who paid good money for fresh cadavers for study. However, Donnelly's admirers angrily threatened Hall with joining Donnelly's soul in the great boxing ring in the sky unless he returned the body. Hall agreed to give the body back as long as he could retain the right arm – the one that slew the English champion – for medical observation. The arm became an exhibit in a Victorian travelling circus and journeyed around Britain many times, without the rest of Donnelly. The arm eventually made it back to Kilcullen in the 1950s, when publican Jim Byrne gave it a new home in his pub The Hideout, not far from the site of his moment of greatest glory.

In a different century, Dubliner Steve Collins was known as the 'Celtic Warrior' and was at one time WBO middleweight and super-middleweight champion. Collins won twenty-six Irish titles as an amateur before turning professional in Massachusetts, USA in October 1986. His uncle, Jack O'Rourke, was an Irish heavyweight champion in the 1960s and his father was a prize amateur fighter.

In a successful fight against title-holder Chris Eubank, Collins was accused by his opponent of playing mind games. Collins and guru Tony Quinn allowed the press to believe that Collins would be hypnotised for the fight and Collins sat in his corner listening to headphones during Eubanks' ring entrance. During the fight he threw himself around in the manner of one not quite all there.

The retired Collins appeared in the film *Lock, Stock and Two Smoking Barrels* in 1998 as a boxing gym bouncer.

CYCLISTS DUBLINERS CYCLING FOR IRELAND

Stephen Roche
In a 13-year professional career that peaked in 1987, Dubliner Stephen Roche was the second of only two cyclists to win the Triple Crown of victories in the Tour de France and the Giro d'Italia stage races, plus the World road race championship. He had fifty-eight professional career wins.

Dervla Murphy
Touring cyclist Dervla Murphy, who was born of Dublin parents in Waterford, is best known for her 1965 book *Full Tilt: Ireland to India With a Bicycle* about an overland cycling trip through Europe, Iran, Afghanistan, Pakistan and India. Murphy travelled alone and unaided, depending on the hospitality of local people. However, she

described her worst incident as tripping over her cats at home and shattering her left arm.

Paul Kimmage

Dublin-born Paul Kimmage was road race champion of Ireland in 1981 and represented Ireland at the 1984 Summer Olympics in Los Angeles, California. In 1990, Kimmage published *Rough Ride*, detailing his experiences as a domestique, which included references to drug use among competitive cyclists. Kimmage confronted former professional cyclist Lance Armstrong, claiming that most of Armstrong's early US Postal cycling team were doped. Kimmage later became an Irish sports journalist, writing for *The Sunday Times*. In 2012, he was named among the top ten most influential sportswriters in Britain by the trade publication, *Press Gazette*.

Martin Earley

In 1986 Martin Earley won the fourteenth stage of the Giro d'Italia and the second of the Tour of the Basque Country. The Dubliner turned professional in 1985 with the Fagor team. The highlight of his career was a stage win in the 1989 Tour de France when he broke clear of three riders 750m from the end of 157km from Labastide-d'Armagnac to Pau. He switched to mountain biking, riding for Raleigh and then for individual sponsors. Earley competed in the 1996 Olympic Games in Atlanta in the mountain bike race and finished 25th.

SOCCER'S DUBLIN HEAD-THE-BALLS

Today, the Republic of Ireland national football team represents Ireland in association football. The team plays its home fixtures at the Aviva Stadium in Dublin, which used to be called Lansdowne Road Stadium, where, at one time, it was quite difficult to beat the Irish soccer team.

As a national side, the team made its debut at the 1924 Summer Olympics, reaching the quarterfinals. Between then and 1936, the team competed as the Irish Free State and from then until 1950 it was known as Éire, or Ireland. In 1953, the international body that

regulates these things, FIFA, said the national team would be called the Republic of Ireland, which was nice and long as a name, but did not really help to score more goals.

Nonetheless, under the guidance of Jack Charlton and his successor Mick McCarthy, Captain Fantastic, the team enjoyed its most successful era, qualifying for UEFA Euro 1988 in a first appearance at the UEFA European Championship. It reached the quarterfinals of the 1990 FIFA World Cup, in its first-ever appearance at the finals. The players also made it to the final sixteen at both the 1994 and 2002 FIFA World Cups. Every time they came home after being knocked out of the competitions, the people went wild and celebrated all over the place; just because they had done so well, and were Irish; and played in Dublin when they weren't away foreign.

After Charlton left his position, the team travelled along unexcitedly, until, under the guidance of Giovanni Trapattoni, the team narrowly lost out (again) on qualification for the 2010 FIFA World Cup during a controversial play-off. Ireland went out to France on an aggregate score of 2–1 that has riled Irishmen ever since. French striker Thierry Henry later admitted he had intentionally handled the ball without the referee seeing the foul to set up William Gallas's decisive goal against Ireland. Ireland went on to qualify for UEFA Euro 2012, but did not win the competition. The team qualified for the 2014 FIFA World Cup when they were grouped with Germany, Sweden, Kazakhstan, Austria and the Faroe Islands, but were knocked out once more, which led to the departure of Trapattoni.

GALLOPING HORSES

Horace Rochford founded the All Ireland Polo Club, said to be the oldest polo club in the world, in 1873 and the club has played on the Nine Acre field in Phoenix Park, Dublin, ever since. In 1893, the reported attendance at one tournament was 15,000 and by 1909, there were an estimated 30,000 watching the riders compete. But, when cinema and then television came along not so many people turned up to watch the galloping. Nonetheless, Polo is still played there three times a week in the summer.

In another horsey context, some professional trainers of racehorses used a designated gallop across the Fifteen Acres in Phoenix Park to train racehorses. Though the gallop, running from west to east on the southern side of the Fifteen Acres, is still there, it has fallen into disuse. Most of the stables in the surrounding countryside moved away to quieter areas of the country, as building development suffocated the leafy lanes around the park.

The first Dublin Horse Show was held in 1864 when there were 366 entries, with a total prize fund of £520. In an admirable show of inclusivity, ass and mule classes were included at the first show. In 1870, the show combined with an Annual Sheep Show, which was also admirable.

Original rules for the show jumping or leaping competitions were simple: the obstacles had to be cleared to the satisfaction of the judges, although whatever might have satisfied a judge in those days we do not know. Females were not allowed to ride in any jumping competition until 1919, when a novelty class for women was introduced. Though, by 1920 women were able to compete freely in competition. Since then, shows have been held annually, except during the two world wars in 1914–19 and 1940–46.

CROSSHEAD 10 SWIMMING IN THE LIFFEY

The annual Liffey Swim starts at Watling Street Bridge beside Collins Barracks Museum. It normally takes competitors past the Four Courts, under the Ha'penny Bridge to finish somewhere around the Customs House. The average entry is 200 males and 80 females. Wetsuits are not allowed, and even though the race takes place in August or early September it can still be cold.

The section of the river where the swimming takes place is tidal, so, depending on tidal flows, race times vary from one year to the next. However, in 2012 and 2013, because of development of a new light rail bridge from Hawkins Street to Malborough Street, the race was shortened and moved downstream from the historic route. Instead it started at Butt Bridge, beside the Customs House, and finished at a pontoon on the north side of the river, beside the East Link Bridge in front of the Point Theatre, which was renamed the O2, but not for the race. That had to do with advertising and branding the old railway station as a concert venue, nothing to do with swimming at all.

On the other hand, Forty Foot promontory sticks out of Dublin Bay at Sandycove, County Dublin, from which people have been swimming in the Irish Sea all year round for some 250 years, though not competitively.

It was kept solely as a gentlemen's bathing place for donkey's years. A gentlemen's swimming club was established to help conserve the area. As a result, it became a popular spot for nude gentlemen to swim in. Then, in the 1970s, some female, equal-rights activists plunged into the waters in defiance of the startled men.

It is now open to women and children as well as to men to swim there.

6

LEISURE AND ENTERTAINMENT

A NOTE FOR THE CONFUSED

Various locations are listed below, but the postal districts may confuse the uninitiated. Dubliners mostly ignore them, except when posting Christmas cards to people they have otherwise forgotten or in ignoring letters posted by creditors.

The General Post Office is on O'Connell Street, Dublin 1, wherefrom all else radiates. The odd numbers relate to areas north of the Liffey; even numbers refer to areas south of the river. County Dublin relates to many disparate places: ask locally for directions. Phoenix Park is designated as Dublin 8, although it is located on the north side of the river. However, the sorting office for post for the park was on the south side – in Dublin 8 – so that's what the postal address is. Farmleigh House is listed as being in Phoenix Park, which it is not, it merely abuts the park, although the Office of Public Works owns both properties on behalf of the nation. However, because Farmleigh House's official entrance lies on Castleknock Road, it is in Dublin 15. So post to Farmleigh House is to be sent to Dublin 15, where it is, and not to Dublin 8, where it or Phoenix Park is not. Simple really.

GUINNESS STOREHOUSE

Arthur Guinness was born upstream of his brewery in 1725, near Celbridge, in the neighbouring county of Kildare. He died a long time ago, but the work goes on – Arthur signed a 9,000-year lease for the production site beside the Liffey in 1759, so it will remain there for a few more years.

The Storehouse, erected between 1902 and 1904, was the most visited tourist attraction in the entire country in 2012; more than a million people (the actual number was 1,087,209) called in to gaze at it all in wonder. It was once the fermentation plant of the brewery and is now remodelled into a visitor centre, dedicated to the history of Guinness and its doings, even though Diageo, a different outfit to the original Guinness, now owns the place. The Storehouse housed the largest tun (large wooden vessels made of oak or pine that hold fermenting beer) in the world, which had a capacity of 7,800 barrels of beer, and in 1960, the overall capacity of the Storehouse was 39,300 barrels.

Visitors to the Storehouse can learn how to pour a pint of Guinness, if they are so inclined, and enjoy 360-degree panoramic views over Dublin from the windows of the Gravity Bar; not at the same time, lest there be spillage.

Today, some three million pints of Guinness are brewed every day at the St James's Gate brewery. Which is a lot of swallowing.

St James Gate, Dublin 8 / 01 4084800 / www.guinness-storehouse.com

DUBLIN ZOO

Dublin Zoo was established in 1831 when the ruling Lord Lieutenant granted the new Zoological Society use of a portion of Phoenix Park for the purpose of creating a menagerie. However, the zoological gardens of the 1830s were nothing like it is today. On opening day there was just one wild boar to be seen – in its day an undomesticated boar would have been a wild and exotic creature to see. It still would, if it was loose. Other species followed and today's visitor may see some 400 animals across more than 60 acres of the modern zoo.

Dublin Zoo was Ireland's second most popular place to visit in 2012, according to visitor numbers, which were recorded at 1,029,417. The Dublin establishment is part of a worldwide network of zoos working together to breed endangered species. Studbooks are used to manage this captive breeding programme and Dublin Zoo

holds the European studbooks for species, including the Moluccan cockatoo and the golden lion tamarin.

Visitors can do lots of things at the zoo. In addition to viewing animals as animals view them back they can also take tea and get married, though advance booking is required for marriages of humans.

Phoenix Park, Dublin / 8 01 474 89 00 / www.dublinzoo.ie

BOOK OF KELLS, DUBLIN – 561-259

The Book of Kells is a ninth-century illuminated manuscript written in Latin. Taking its name from the Abbey of Kells in County Meath (its home for many centuries), the Book of Kells was created by monks and is considered a masterwork of Western calligraphy. It is also widely regarded as Ireland's finest national treasure.

The decoration combines traditional Christian iconography with the ornate swirling motifs typical of insular art. Figures of humans, animals and mythical beasts, together with Celtic knots and interlacing patterns in vibrant colours, enliven the manuscript's pages. The manuscript comprises 340 folios and, since 1953, has been bound in four volumes. Its leaves are on high-quality calf vellum and the text appears to be the work of at least three different scribes, according to experts. Iron gall ink was used to create the lettering and the colours used were derived from a wide range of substances.

The book is on permanent display at Trinity College Library, which displays two of the current four volumes at a time – one showing a major illustration and the other showing typical text pages, so it would take you a long time to read it all. Trinity College is the oldest university in Ireland and beside the Book of Kells, it houses a number of other treasures including the Books of Durrow and Armagh and an early Irish harp – though playing of the harp is not allowed.

College Street, Dublin 2 / 01 8962320 / www.bookofkells.ie

ST PATRICK'S CATHEDRAL

Built in honour of Ireland's patron saint, St Patrick's Cathedral – the National Cathedral of the Church of Ireland – stands adjacent to the well, where tradition has it that St Patrick baptized converts on his visit to Dublin.

The parish church of St Patrick was granted collegiate status on this site in 1191 and raised to cathedral status in 1224; the present building dates from 1220. By 1509, one of the first public clocks in Dublin was installed in the tower, raising the cathedral to equal status of public building as Dublin Castle. The time on the cathedral is shown on two copper dials, 8ft in diameter, on the west and north-facing sides of the tower.

Jonathan Swift, author and journalist, was dean of St Patrick's Cathedral from 1713.

Saint Patrick's Close, Dublin 8 / 01 4754817 / www.stpatrickscathedrat.ie

KILMAINHAM GAOL

First built in 1796, Kilmainham Gaol was the official County of Dublin Gaol and is now one of the largest, unoccupied gaols in Europe. That is, it has no prisoners, but lots of people pay money to go in and take a look about. It is most famous for being the execution place of the leaders of the 1916 Uprising that led to Irish independence.

Hanging was a common punishment for all sorts of crimes and public hangings took place at the front of the gaol where people gathered to watch the death throes of the condemned person. A small hanging cell was built inside the gaol in 1891, where you at least were afforded some privacy in your final minutes of life. Prisoners were not segregated and men, women and children were incarcerated up to five in each cell, with only a single candle (replaced once a fortnight) for light and heat. Many children arrested for petty theft were lodged in Kilmainham with adults until they were dispersed to various reformatories situated around the country. A lot of the adult prisoners who were not hanged were transported to Australia.

Kilmainham Gaol was decommissioned as a prison by the first Irish Free State government in 1924. Today, the building houses a major exhibition detailing the political and penal history of the prison and its inmates. A tour of the prison includes an audio-visual show, but no re-enacted executions.

Inchicore Road, Kilmainham, Dublin 8 / 01 4535984 / www.heritageireland.ie/en/Dublin/Kilmainham

NATIONAL GALLERY OF IRELAND

The National Gallery of Ireland first opened its doors to the public on 30 January 1864. It was said that desire had been raised by the masses for such a gallery following a spectacular exhibition on Leinster Lawn in June 1852, which was facilitated by William Dargan, the father of the Irish rail network. The opening collection comprised 112 pictures, including thirty that were on loan from the National Gallery in London and elsewhere.

In 1866, an annual purchase grant of £1,000 was allocated for the acquisition of pictures to display. Today, the collection includes more than 2,500 paintings and some 10,000 other works in different media, including watercolours, drawings and sculpture dating from the early thirteenth century through to the mid-twentieth century. Every major European school of painting is represented. The collection boasts an impressive range of masterpieces by artists from the major European schools of art, whilst also featuring the world's most comprehensive collection of Irish art, according to the Gallery. Highlights include works by Vermeer, Caravaggio, Picasso, Van Gogh and Jack B. Yeats.

In January 2002, the Millennium Wing opened, which was two years late for a real millennium nomenclature, but was a catchy title nonetheless. Designed by London-based architects Benson & Forsyth and located on sites purchased by the gallery a decade earlier, the new wing introduced a second public entrance to the gallery from an adjacent busy thoroughfare, which in one swoop gave people in two places the opportunity to be in the same place at the same time.

Clare Street, Dublin 2 / 01 6615133 / www.nationalgallery.ie

NATIONAL BOTANIC GARDENS

In 1790, the Irish Parliament, with the active support of John Foster, the Speaker of the House, granted funds to the Dublin Society – later the Royal Dublin Society – to establish a public botanic garden, and in 1795 the gardens were founded on lands at Glasnevin. It was opened to the public in 1805.

As well as having aesthetic appeal, the National Botanic Gardens in Glasnevin is noted for its fine plant collections that are of scientific interest, holding more than 15,000 plant species and cultivars from a variety of habitats from all around the world. It is also renowned for its exquisitely restored and planted glasshouses, notably the Turner Curvilinear Range and the Great Palm House. Both were recipients of the Europa Nostra award for excellence in conservation architecture. The east wing's central dome featured for many years on Irish stamps.

Home to more than 300 endangered plant species from around the world, visitors to the gardens may enjoy herbaceous borders, a rose garden, an alpine yard, pond area, rock garden and arboretum.

Glasnevin, Dublin 9 / 01 8040300 / www.botanicgardens.ie

NATIONAL MUSEUM OF ARCHAEOLOGY

Opened in 1890, the museum is the national repository for all archaeological objects found in Ireland and home to more than 2 million artefacts, dating from 7,000 BC – that's a lot of bits and bobs that people have dug up.

All archaeological objects found in Ireland that have no known owner are State property, so you cannot keep anything of archaeological value that you find with a metal detector or a well-aimed fork. Finders are obliged to report their discoveries to the National Museum of Ireland – rewards are paid in respect of discoveries, so there's always that. As a consequence, the core collection continues to grow rapidly, mainly as a result of large-scale archaeological excavation.

Collections include the finest prehistoric gold artefacts in Western Europe, outstanding examples of metalwork from the Celtic Iron Age and a world-renowned collection of medieval objects and jewellery. The Broighter Hoard, Ardagh Chalice, Tara Brooch and Derrynaflan Hoard are among the masterpieces held by the museum. The Kingship and Sacrifice exhibition centres on a number of recently found bog bodies, though they were in the ground for a long time and have no next of kin – that anyone knows about. The museum also houses a rich collection of Egyptian and Viking material.

Kildare Street, Dublin 2 / 01 677 44 44 / www.museum.ie

FARMLEIGH HOUSE

Artillery units of the Irish Army fired at Farmleigh House on the western perimeter of Phoenix Park in the late summer of 2001. Smoke drifted across the 78 acres of gardens and rolling lawns while onlookers cheered the booming of the guns. No damage was caused, however, as the artillery was firing blanks to supply the cannon effect for Tchaikovsky's *1812 Overture*, performed by RTÉ's Symphony Orchestra, after Taoiseach Bertie Ahern TD, in the company of 8,000 invited guests, formally opened the nineteenth-century house as the State's first official guesthouse.

An offer to sell Farmleigh at €19.05 million was declined by the Irish Government in 1998, but a year later the Office of Public Works (OPW) bought the house and grounds from the Guinness family for €29.20 million, on behalf of the State. Much-needed renovation, refurbishment and upgrading brought the bill to €52 million; which was a bargain, according to Martin Cullen TD, Junior Minister for the Environment, who was in charge of the purchase and renovation.

The Benjamin Iveagh collection of rare books, bindings and manuscripts is held in the Library at Farmleigh.

Phoenix Park Dublin 15 / 01 8155900 / www.farmleigh.ie

SCIENCE GALLERY

It was projected that a new science gallery in Dublin, that would house visiting exhibitions on high-tech clothing, robots, neuro science and light art, would attract some 50,000 visitors in its first year. A rather modest estimation, as it turn out, because in the space of five years, more than a million visitors poured in to the Science Gallery city centre space, which opened its doors in 2008.

Unlike most galleries, there is no permanent collection, which means, according to the administrators, that there is always something new to see. However, between exhibitions, only the shop and café remain open, so, as with everything to do with science, timing is everything.

Many of its exhibitions feature hands-on visitor participation, which attract many families. The gallery offers two floors of interactive exhibitions, with changing focus on different areas of science.

In 2011, the Science Gallery received a gift from Google to launch the Global Science Gallery Network: a network of eight Science Gallery locations to be developed in partnership with leading universities in urban centres worldwide by 2020.

The Naughton Institute, Pearse Street, Trinity College, Dublin 2 / 01 896 4091 / https://sciencegallery.com

NATURAL HISTORY MUSEUM

The Natural History Museum, also known as the Dead Zoo, features galleries of animals from Ireland and overseas and geological exhibits from a total collection of some 2 million

scientific specimens. The free-admission museum is stuffed full of glass cases, which, in turn, are full of animals that were stuffed in the nineteenth century. Upper floors house lots of expired animals from an armadillo to a zebra. There is even a 20m-long whale skeleton suspended from the roof for visitors to gaze up at in awe – viewed by some as a preferable perspective to its live equivalent leaping across your boat at sea. You can also stare at a tiger through its glass eye, or get close and personal with a deceased giraffe.

In addition to its continuing exhibits, the museum celebrates seasonal festivals with activities to mark numerous occasions: Darwin Day in February; Seachtain Na Gaeilge in March; Biodiversity Month and Bealtaine in May; Heritage Week in August; Science Week and Culture Night in September.

Natural History, Dublin Merrion Street, Dublin 2 / 01 6777444 / www.museum.ie

NATIONAL MUSEUM OF IRELAND DECORATIVE ARTS AND HISTORY

Collins Barracks used to be the oldest barracks in the world until it closed down and was de-commissioned in 1997, when it became part of the National Museum of Ireland. It now holds silver, ceramics, glassware, weaponry, furniture, folk life exhibits, clothing, jewellery, coins and medals.

More than 1,000 objects from all over the world cover 1,700 square metres of the old barracks, as the Soldiers and Chiefs exhibition traces Ireland's military history, both at home and abroad, from 1550 and into the twenty-first century. There is also a permanent exhibition that examines the decade of disturbance between 1913 and 1923, from the Dublin Lockout, through the Easter Rising and to the end of the Civil War. An original copy of the Proclamation of the Republic, as read by Pádraig Pearse outside the General Post Office on Easter Monday, 1916, occupies a central position in the exhibition. Remains of revolutionaries of an earlier rebellion are buried in the Croppie's Acre outside the barracks complex.

In the late twentieth century, a curious proposal to cover over the burial area for coach parking for visitors to the museum was opposed and defeated without a further uprising by the fallen dead.

Benburb Street, Dublin 7 / 01 6777444 / www.museum.ie

CHESTER BEATTY LIBRARY

The Chester Beatty Library shows you what you can do when you have a passion for collecting and the cash to finance it. The art museum and library houses a vast collection of manuscripts, miniature paintings, prints, rare books and decorative arts assembled by Sir Alfred Chester Beatty, who expired in 1968 when he left it all behind him. Before that, Beatty was an Irish-American mining magnate and millionaire. In fact, he was often called the 'King of Copper', though he was not known to be of royal blood. He was naturalised as British in 1933, knighted by the British in 1954 and then made an honorary citizen of Ireland in 1957. On his death in 1968, Beatty was accorded a State funeral by the Irish Government – one of the few private citizens in Irish history to receive such an honour. He is buried in Glasnevin Cemetery in Dublin.

The library used to be on Shrewsbury Road, the most expensive road in the Irish version of Monopoly, but it was moved to Dublin Castle in 2000, where it remains. The library's rich collections from countries across Asia, the Middle East, North Africa and Europe includes Egyptian papyrus texts, illuminated copies of the Qur'an, the Bible, and European medieval and Renaissance manuscripts. In its diversity, the collection includes works for 2700 BC to the present day.

Dublin Castle, Dublin 2 / 01 4070750 / www.cbl.ie

NATIONAL LIBRARY OF IRELAND

Home of the most comprehensive compilation of Irish documentary material in the world, the National Library of Ireland includes in its Dublin city collection music, periodicals, photographs, maps, manuscripts and genealogical material.

The library does not lend books; instead, reading is done in various reading rooms. However, beware that such research is addictive and may lead to bleary eyes from reading too much, for too long. The library also has an on-going programme of exhibitions.

Kildare Street, Dublin 2 / 01 6030200 / www.nli.ie

WINDMILL LANE RECORDING STUDIOS

In 2013, a recording studio, which hosted recording sessions by U2, Depeche Mode and The Rolling Stones, issued an appeal to the musicians who worked there to collect their master tapes, or else they would be destroyed – the tapes that is, not the musicians.

U2 made many of their early albums in Windmill Lane Recording Studios, but they probably made sure to keep their masters in a safe place. The Spice Girls, The Chieftains and AC/DC also recorded there, although not at the same time.

The studio placed some of the artefacts on display and encouraged enthusiasts and fans to drop in to pay a visit to see the nostalgic pieces all in one place, for a final time.

The studio, which was set up in 1978, has since relocated from Windmill Lane to new premises, but the old studio remains a site of pilgrimage for fans visiting the much-graffitied U2 wall, where people can write things about Dublin-based band, U2. Writing on the wall began when fans used to hang around Windmill Lane in Dublin's dockside area in the hope of seeing band members enter or leave the studio, and whilst waiting, they wrote on the wall – as you do. Inside the studio, meanwhile, musicians and technicians got on with the business of recording music that those outside would hope to buy for their personal listening.

PHOENIX PARK

Phoenix Park was the home of the three most powerful men in Ireland under British rule: Lord Lieutenant or Viceroy, Chief Secretary and Under Secretary, all of whom dwelt within a stone's throw of one another. The park is now home to the President of Ireland and the Ambassador of the United States. The Phoenix Park Visitor Centre was also a residence, until a few years ago, to the Papal Nuncio, the representative of the Vatican in Ireland. However, the Papal Nuncio moved out ahead of the announcement that dry rot had infested the building. When the building was pulled down, a fifteenth-century keep was discovered inside the old building, which is now part of the modern Visitor Centre.

The park is a large, enclosed area of 1,752 acres and within its walls you'll find both passive and active recreational facilities. For sports people there are organised games and activities, as well as open expanses for others to engage in solitary sports. For the romantic, there are paths and woods to explore and for families there are the myriad wonders of Dublin Zoo with which to while away the hours.

An exhibition on the history and the wildlife of Phoenix Park is on display in the Visitor Centre, which also houses a restaurant within its grounds.

Dublin 8 / 01 6770095 / www.phoenixparkbook.com

DUBLIN CITY GALLERY THE HUGH LANE

Dublin City Gallery The Hugh Lane was originally called The Municipal Gallery of Modern Art and opened in January 1908 in temporary premises in Harcourt Street, Dublin; it is now located on historic Parnell Square in the heart of the city.

The original collection – donated by the gallery's founder, Sir Hugh Lane, in 1908 – has grown to include more than 2,000 artworks, ranging from the Impressionist masterpieces of Manet, Monet, Renoir and Degas, to works by leading national and international contemporary artists.

Sadly, Lane did not live to see his gallery permanently located, as he perished in 1915 aboard the RMS *Lusitania*, when it was sunk off the west coast of Cork by a torpedo from a German submarine during the First World War.

Lane's will bequeathed his collection to London, but a later un-witnessed codicil bequeathed it to Dublin; however, London's National Gallery did not recognise the codicil and an argument ensued. Many years of negotiation followed until it was agreed in 1993 that thirty-one of the thirty-nine paintings would stay in Ireland. The remaining eight were divided into two groups, so that four would be lent for six years at a time to Dublin. In 2008, the National Gallery in London arranged for the entire collection to be on display in Dublin together for the first time.

The Hugh Lane Gallery was enhanced in 1998, with the acquisition of the entire contents of Dublin-born Francis Bacon's studio, donated by Bacon's sole heir: John Edwards. The studio, located at 7 Reece Mews, London, was relocated in its entirety to Dublin.

Outside the gallery, and almost as a come-on, is a Julian Opie work featuring *Suzanne Walking*. The bright orange LED light display on the forecourt of the gallery is seen by thousands of Dubliners as they pass by. She walks forever, never quite leaving, never returning.

Parnell Square North Dublin 1 / 01 222 55 50 / www.hughlane.ie

DUBLIN WRITERS MUSEUM

Two buildings that are devoted to Irish writing stand cheek by jowl on Parnell Square: the Irish Writers Centre and the splendidly restored eighteenth-century townhouse that became home, in 1991, to the Dublin Writers Museum. Further down the street stands the Hugh Lane Gallery and plans are afoot by the powers-that-be to further develop this area of the city as an arts quarter.

In the museum, Dublin's literary celebrities from the past 300 years are brought to life through their books, letters, portraits and personal items, providing an introduction to an extraordinary literary tradition. Otherwise, books are shown that represent milestones in Irish literature including *Gulliver's Travels*, *Dracula*, *The Importance of Being Earnest*, *Ulysses* and *Waiting for Godot*. Most of these are first or early editions, recapturing the moment when they surprised their first reader. Objects that belonged to Dublin writers are also on display, from Samuel Beckett's telephone and Brendan Behan's typewriter to Mary Lavin's teddy bear.

18 Parnell Square North, Dublin 1 / 01 8722077 / www.writersmuseum.com

IRISH MUSEUM OF MODERN ART

The Irish Museum of Modern Art is housed in the Royal Hospital Kilmainham. James Butler, Duke of Ormonde and Viceroy to Charles II, founded the Royal Hospital in 1684 as a home for retired soldiers – many of the invalid soldiers provided a sentry guard across the river at the magazine fort and veterans named the road below them as the Khyber Pass, a name that has applied to Khyber Road ever since.

The style of the building is based on Les Invalides in Paris, with a formal façade and a large elegant courtyard (the Royal Hospital in Chelsea was completed two years later, in 1686, and contains many similarities in style). Earlier than this, a hospital was founded on the site by the Norman invader, Strongbow. It was under the care of the Knights of St John of Jerusalem, but was demolished in 1670. The site was also once included in an area that became Phoenix Park, though the modern park is now restrained inside a wall on the far bank of the River Liffey.

The seventeenth-century building was restored in 1984 and opened as the Irish Museum of Modern Art in May 1991. Exhibitions are mounted in the rooms and corridors of the old hospital to some effect and are never less than interesting. Aside from a place to see modern art, the grounds are occasionally the venue for open-air concerts and circuses.

Military Road, Kilmainham, Dublin 8 / 01 612 99 00 / www.imma.ie

THE JAMES JOYCE CENTRE

Situated in a beautifully restored Georgian townhouse near Parnell Square, the James Joyce Centre houses a permanent exhibition, including: educational installations and video documentaries; a copy of Joyce's death mask; furniture from Paul Leon's Paris apartment, where Joyce wrote *Finnegan's Wake*; and the front door from Number 7 Eccles Street, the home of Leopold Bloom in *Ulysses*. Except that Bloom was a fictional character and the door is real, but the story goes that Joyce knew the door in real life and included it in his book as a consequence. Welcome to Dublin literature and reality.

The centre operates popular walking tours throughout the year of

Joyce's Dublin, as well as a comprehensive programme of activities, including the annual Bloomsday Festival, which attracts literary pilgrims from across the globe each June. *Ulysses* – the novel that provided the inspiration for the festival – is set on 16 June, a usually fine day for a walk around Dublin, on which Joyce (the real person) first stepped out with Nora Barnacle (the real person) on a date. Joyce and Barnacle went off out of Ireland early in his writing career and Joyce spent his time elsewhere writing about his home town, making sure of his accuracy of streetscape description by asking visitors to describe bits and pieces of Dublin to him when they met him in self-imposed exile.

For many years afterwards many (mostly male) writers tried, unsuccessfully, to emulate Joyce in their writing. But not so much now. Edwardian straw hats may be purchased in the museum to wear, if that helps you with writing like Joyce.

35 North Great George's Street, Dublin 1 / 01 8788547 / www.jamesjoyce.ie

JEANIE JOHNSON TALL SHIP/ FAMINE MUSEUM

It may seem strange to board a sailing ship in Dublin docks that is going nowhere on the tide and that is, instead, a museum of sail and emigration. However, although in port it is a living history museum on nineteenth-century emigration, the replica *Jeanie Johnston* is also designed as an ocean-going training vessel at sea.

The Jeanie Johnston Tall Ship and Museum enables visitors to see what it was like on board a wooden tall ship during the Famine era of mid-nineteenth-century Ireland. Poverty-stricken Irish emigrants boarded the sturdy ship for the difficult transatlantic voyage and an uncertain future in the New World of America.

The original *Jeanie Johnston* set out on her maiden voyage on 24 April 1848 from Blennerville, County Kerry to Quebec, with 193 passengers on board. Accommodation offered was bare bunks, where four adults shared a 6ft-square space. Over the following seven years the ship carried more than 2,500 emigrants safely to the New World on seven-week journeys in the very cramped and difficult conditions, now replicated on the modern *Jeanie Johnston*. This ship is built with larch planks on oak frames. She also has two Caterpillar engines, two Caterpillar generators, an emergency generator located above the waterline in the forward deckhouse, steel water-tight bulkheads, down-flooding valves and fire-fighting equipment.

During her maiden voyage across the Atlantic in March 2003, she was battered by a force 10 storm in the Bay of Biscay and similarly on the return voyage from Newfoundland in November 2003. Nonetheless, the *Jeanie Johnston* returned unbowed.

Dublin Docklands, Custom House Quay, Dublin 1 / 01 4730111 / www.jeaniejohnston.ie

7

CRIME AND PUNISHMENT

FACTION FIGHTS

Faction fights were pitched battles that occurred all over Ireland in times past, for no good reason that we can discern now other than one lot could boast that they were the best and the others could swear they would be back for revenge.

In one part of Dublin, in Phoenix Park, there is an area known as Butcher's Woods, so-called because of the mayhem caused when butchers from the city markets gathered amongst the trees to settle disputes. More serious disputes and arguments were taken to the park and fought out in ritualised battles with tools of the butchering trade.

In other places, the Liberty Boys (chiefly unemployed weavers) from the south side of the river and the Ormond Boys from the north side fought their way into Dublin folklore. The Ormond Boys were focussed around the fruit and fish markets and drew their numbers from assistants and carriers from slaughter houses. They were also joined by cattle drovers from Smithfield cattle market and various camp followers.

Whenever word was received of a set-to among the protagonists, a body of soldiers would attempt to disperse the fighters. They were often obliged to fire on the fighters before they could put them to flight. Shooting to kill was considered a better alternative to the trouble and expense of imprisoning them and bringing them to trial. Group counselling was unheard of at that time.

HELL

Not far from Christ Church Cathedral was a place called Hell. It can be visited still, though it has cooled down somewhat. This was a real place, not a notional article of faith.

Before the present-day Four Courts was built, the old Four Courts of Chancery, Exchequer, Kings Bench and Common Pleas adjoined Christ Church Cathedral until 1797, when the new buildings across the river opened for business.

Hell was the name given to a narrow cobbled laneway between the courts and the cathedral. Over its arched entrance there was the image of the devil, carved in oak, since taken down and used for other purposes. Hell is said to have included workplaces and living places for those whose business was the courts. There are others that claim that an element of support services was supplied by well-meaning souls that were more usually found in Monto, a red light district across the river.

Hell was bordered by Winetavern Street and Fishamble Street, where Handel's *Messiah* was first performed, and where fishmongers discarded their cut-offs from fish they sold to fussy customers on the roadway. This practice brought complaints from those on the road to Hell and those already there, who, as you might expect, did not want to be slipping on fish heads on the street.

The place quietened down after the legal people and their clients and camp followers migrated across to the new buildings a year before the 1798 uprising – an event that brought more work to the lawyers, as unsuccessful revolutionaries appeared before the courts on their way to another life experience somewhere else – perhaps even Hell.

NEW COURTS BUILDING

The gallows for Dublin County once stood where the new Courts of Criminal Justice now stand at Parkgate Street. Those sentenced to death were hanged publicly there. The gallows was moved to Kilmainham in the seventeenth century to make room for a large dog kennel at the entrance to the new Phoenix Park (the kennel was large and was for many dogs, rather than a single kennel for a very large animal). Defendants arriving before the law since 2010, when the new courts building opened, are, therefore, spared the sight of the noose on their way in to answer to charges.

The current building was designed to deal with criminal business of Dublin District Court, Dublin Circuit Court, Central Criminal Court, Special Criminal Court and Court of Criminal Appeal. Light is filtered into the courtrooms by means of an external bronze screen, which highlights the walnut furniture and fittings; which is nice if you are not the defendant when such finery doesn't matter to you, so much.

The current building provides separate and secure segregation for the public, jurors, persons in custody, judiciary and staff. The eleven-story building has more than 450 rooms, including twenty-two courtrooms, so there's a lot of lawyering going on at any given moment. There is cell accommodation for 100 prisoners, together with a prison reception area, prison officer accommodation and ancillary facilities.

HANG 'EM HIGH

Capital punishment has been abolished in the Republic of Ireland for a good many years now. The last person to be executed was Michael Manning in 1954 for the rape and murder of Catherine Cooper, a nurse. Manning was hanged in Mountjoy Prison in Dublin; the hang house in Mountjoy stood next to the condemned cell.

As capital punishment declined there was no trained Irish hangman available to execute people and the English hangman, Albert Pierrepoint, had to travel over by sea to dispatch the condemned person. From 1954 until 1990 every death sentence that was passed was commuted by the Irish president, within whose power that judgment lay, even though capital punishment remained on the statute book. The death penalty was finally abolished in law in 1990 and has been specifically prohibited by the Constitution of Ireland since 2002. Under the constitution, a penalty of death cannot be reintroduced, even in war or a state of emergency. Now, the penalty for treason and first-degree murder is life imprisonment, with parole in not less than forty years.

In earlier times, by contrast, Gibbet's Glade, located somewhere around modern-day Arbour Hill, was a place of public execution for criminals. Being hanged from a gibbet usually meant the dead body was left to hang in the air for as long as the authorities saw fit, as a warning to all. Sometimes, the deceased swung there until their clothes rotted away; sometimes they swung until the body decomposed. People said it made a mournful sound when a dead man swung in the wind, waiting for his body to rot, while crows pecked away at what was left.

If a person was not left hanging from a gibbet, it was the custom of the hangman to toss the dead bodies of his charges into a nearby pit beside the place of execution.

DUBLIN
METROPOLITAN POLICE

While the new metropolitan district was being laid out in Dublin in the 1800s, law and order in general around the country was maintained by constables and watchmen employed by local authorities, supported by British military forces. Chief Secretary Robert Peel sponsored a law in 1816, creating a basic police force organised along paramilitary lines. In 1836, county and provincial constabularies were merged into a centralised constabulary.

From its formation in 1836 until 1922, the Dublin Metropolitan Police Force (DMP), with their distinctive pointed helmets, functioned as an unarmed force. The Royal Irish Constabulary (RIC) – a paramilitary force armed with carbines and bayonets – policed the rest of the country.

On independence in 1922, responsibility for the force was taken over by the Free State Government and it was re-named Póilíní Áth Cliath. The DMP was amalgamated with the new, also unarmed, Garda Síochána force in April 1925 and moved to Phoenix Park from its own depot in Kevin Street at the rear of St Patrick's Cathedral, where a modern Garda station now stands. In the early 1930s, the pointed helmets of the city policemen were replaced by the familiar flat cap of today, though some pointed helmets are to be seen in photographs of a subsequent era, so some overlap seems to have occurred.

The Irish Constabulary was awarded the prefix Royal by Queen Victoria for suppressing the Fenian Rising in 1867. The royal accolade survived in the Royal Ulster Constabulary until 2001, when that force was renamed the Police Service of Northern Ireland.

Members of the RIC were brought into Dublin to assist the city police during the 1913 Lockout. They were involved in the infamous attack on protestors on O'Connell Street on Sunday 31 August. A number of people were killed by police violence over that weekend, an occurrence still recalled by modern Dubliners.

BREHON LAW

Long before the English conquest and subsequent imposition of English law across Ireland, Brehon law was the law observed among the Irish, surviving until the seventeenth century, when it was finally replaced by English common law. Until then, English law was confined to an area known as the Pale, which was made up of Dublin, its hinterland and the east coast. Beyond the Pale, Brehon law continued to be applied.

Brehon law passed orally from one generation to the next. It was not until the seventh century that the laws were written down for the first time.

More arbitrators than punishing judges, the task of Brehon administrators was to preserve and interpret the law, rather than expand it. Restitution before punishment was prescribed for wrongdoing and homicide or bodily injury was punishable by means of fine, the exact amount being determined by a scale. Capital punishment was not practised under Brehon laws – in any case, there was neither a court system nor a police force to uphold such administration, as Brehon law functioned by consent. The laws recognised divorce and equal rights between male and female, which, if not making everyone happy, was at least fair.

The change from Brehon law to English law began in the sixteenth century when King Henry VIII implemented a scheme of surrender and re-grant of land held by native noble families, which brought them within the feudal system of land tenure and assisted the spread of English law. The end of Brehon law authority finally came with the Proclamation of King James I in 1603, which received the Irish people into the King's protection. English law was administered throughout the country, thereafter. Or ignored by the populace as much as possible.

CHURCH ARSON

A homeless man was found not guilty, by reason of insanity, of the arson of a Dublin city-centre church on 2 January 2012. The blaze caused more than 4 million euro's worth of damage, but it was not his fault, his people said.

The man admitted setting fire to straw behind a crib in the church with his lighter. He said he had done it because he was God Almighty and, furthermore, he had told witnesses in a nearby hairdressers that he was 'off to Rome to burn out the paedophiles'. On arrival at the Garda station with arresting officers, the accused signed his fingerprint consent forms as Jesus Christ.

A consultant psychiatrist at the Central Mental Hospital gave evidence for the defence that he was of the opinion that, at the time of the offence, the accused was suffering from a mental illness such that he was unable to refrain from carrying out the act. The jury of seven men and five women returned their verdict on the second day of the trial following 65 minutes of deliberation.

Following the acquittal, Judge Desmond Hogan ordered a psychiatric evaluation to assess the man's need for long-term care, as required by The Criminal Law Insanity Act 2006.

HAPLESS ASSASSIN SHOOTS HIMSELF

To be a successful assassin you need two essentials: the ability to kill and the ability to escape. However, when a would-be killer targeted a Dublin man in the suburb of Glasnevin in 2013, he ended up wounding his victim and then shooting himself by mistake.

Charles O'Neill (52) from nearby Ballymun, who was known locally as 'The Walrus,' but in this case acquired a nomenclature of 'The Victim', was cycling along a morning rush hour road when the killer stepped out and discharged a shotgun at him, according to reports at the scene. It was just after 8 a.m. at a bus stop, where city commuters were waiting to go to work or school or somewhere else, little expecting the drama that was to unfold around them. Shot fired, the assailant then attempted to escape the scene, according to the best assassin's guidelines. Instead, he somehow managed to discharge another round and wound himself in the leg: two down, none to go. Not according to plan A, then. The 31-year-old was found on the ground shortly afterwards by responding gardaí, who were on scene before ambulance crews arrived. Both O'Neill and the injured assailant were taken to separate hospitals, where they were treated for gunshot injuries. Charges followed in court.

THE GREAT GOLD SAFE ROBBERY

Bad enough to fail in a crime caper, but hearing a judge tell you that you rank amongst the all-time stupidest criminals to come before the courts is adding insult to injury.

A 30-year-old man from Edenmore Crescent, Raheny left the scene of a robbery he was involved in at a gold storage business with the keys to the safe, locking the building's shutters behind him. However, in doing so he had inadvertently left his two accomplices trapped inside, along with two staff members who had been tied up during the raid, to await arrest by responding gardaí.

Investigating officers testified that the hapless man was effectively the getaway driver, but he left the scene on Bolton Street alone in the blue Ford courier van the gang had arrived in earlier. He eventually abandoned the van and dumped a hard hat, a high-visibility jacket and purple gloves he had been wearing in the raid. He was later arrested following extensive analysis of CCTV footage. His fingerprints were not only found on the hard hat, but he was also captured on cameras buying the hat on the morning of the robbery.

He was sentenced to seven years in prison after being found guilty of attempted robbery, possession of an imitation firearm and two counts of false imprisonment. However, Judge Donagh McDonagh said he would give him the 'benefit of his stupidity' and suspended the final two years of the sentence after acknowledging that the 30-year-old was not a hardened criminal – which came as no surprise to anyone.

DON'T ROB SWEETS

When three robbers managed to steal only a small amount of cash at a Palmerstown filling station, they decided instead to load up with sweets from the confectionery counter before fleeing on foot. But, like Hansel and Gretel, they left a trail behind them for others to follow. This time it was the pursuing gardaí.

The three fools, after traumatising staff, had grabbed fistfuls of chocolate products as they ran from the premises in the 2 a.m. raid. However, such was their haste, they dropped sweets behind them as they ran into the nearby village. Well-trained gardaí seeking the departed trio soon spotted the trail of fallen confectionary on the ground, which led to the men, who were dividing up the cash spoils of the raid, such as they were. The pursuing officers arrested the surprised robbers, confiscated the sweets and the cash, and took them to a nearby Garda station for more detailed investigation into their inanity.

Back at the crime scene, the shop assistant said he had managed to lock himself inside a room for his own safety when the raiders struck. Nonetheless, he was, not surprisingly, very frightened after the sudden appearance of three men in the station's shop area demanding money.

It is not known whether any of the stolen confectionery was consumed before the pursuit came upon them.

AMERICANS ROBBED A YEAR IN DUBLIN

Each year, some 200 Americans report their passports stolen or lost in Dublin, according to the US Embassy. The area along the banks of the Liffey is popular with pickpockets. Other danger spots are areas frequented by tourists, particularly museums or crowded bus and train stations. Well-dressed pickpockets also operate in hotel restaurants and lobbies and in pubs.

In response, the embassy issued a list of advices to its nationals.

ADVERTISING DOES NOT PAY

Burglars usually attempt to rob the contents of a safe, not the safe itself. However, gardaí caught three crooks trying to do just that in the Dublin suburb of Sundrive Road on St Patrick's Day, 2011, during Cheltenham Race Week, when the safe could be assumed to be full of punters' losses.

As if it was not enough to be apprehended by responding gardaí, one of the criminals threatened to shoot a Garda with a sledgehammer handle that he pretended was a shotgun.

The prosecuting Garda said that when she went to the back of the bookmakers after seeing the burglar alarm flashing, she saw two burglars carrying a safe out into the back of a van. When she shouted at them to stop, one held up a long object and pointed it at her as if it was a shotgun and shouted at her to go away or he would shoot her. The weapon turned out to be a sledgehammer, but at the time the Garda said she believed it was a real firearm and was in fear for her life.

The hapless robbers had used sledgehammers to remove the safe from its concrete housing and had a trolley with them, which they planned to use to move the safe to the van.

Despite their threats, both men surrendered with their hands up. The Garda then found the third man, an apprentice electrician, hiding behind advertising hoarding at the front of the shop.

The three subsequently pleaded guilty to the burglary of Ladbrokes. One, who was already serving a five-year sentence for possession of firearms, also pleaded guilty to threatening to kill gardaí during the burglary and Judge Martin Nolan imposed a two-and-a-half year sentence on him. He sentenced the other two to fifteen months' imprisonment each.

8

BUILDINGS AND PLACES

SMOCK ALLEY THEATRE

Following the austerity of Oliver Cromwell's regime and the Restoration of Charles II in 1660, three major theatres were built in the restored monarch's kingdom: London's Lincoln's Inn Fields in 1661, shortly followed a year later by London's Drury Lane and Dublin's Smock Alley Theatre. Of the three, only Smock Alley exists in substantially the same form as it did in 1662, standing on Lower Exchange Street, just behind Essex Quay. To this day, the original walls may be seen, forming a background to performances.

Smock Alley was Ireland's first Theatre Royal and was opened in 1662 by John Ogilby, Master of the Revels, flourishing for some 150 years. It closed in 1787 and was used as a whiskey store until it was bought by Fr Michael Blake. The building was then converted into a church – the Church of Saints Michael and John, known fondly to Dubliners as Mickey's and Jack's – between 1811 and 1815.

In 1829, history was made there when, after the announcement of Catholic Emancipation, its bell was the first to ring out the Angelus in Dublin since the Reformation, some 300 years earlier.

In 1989, due to falling numbers of parishioners, the Church of Saints Michael and John was deconsecrated. It became the tourist attraction of the 'Viking Adventure', which closed down in 2002. After a six-year renovation, Smock Alley Theatre reopened its doors as Dublin's oldest newest theatre, in May 2012. Its main theatre space is largely as it was when seventeenth-century Dubliners piled in to see the offerings of the day.

OLYMPIA THEATRE

The Olympia Theatre used to have a different name, several in fact. It began life as The Star of Erin and was then renamed Dan Lowrey's Theatre. When Lowrey's closed in 1897, it reopened as The Empire Palace Theatre of Varieties – no false modesty there then. The name changed again, in 1923, to The Olympia Theatre.

The present theatre, a beautiful Rococo building, is almost as it was on that August day in 1897 when it first opened. Almost. In 1974, during a rehearsal break on the opening night of *West Side Story*, the proscenium arch and some of the ceiling above it collapsed, closing the theatre for some time. However, a vigorous public campaign saw the Olympia saved from demolition and it opened its doors again in 1977. A further incident, in 2004, resulted in the outside canopy being struck by a reversing truck, necessitating its removal and reinstatement – the 1897 glass canopy, supported by ornamental pillar and wrought-iron scrollwork, is an icon on Dame Street, in the centre of the city.

World-famous names have appeared at the Olympia, including Charlie Chaplin, Laurel and Hardy, Tyrone Power, Noel Coward, Alec Guinness, Dame Edith Evans, Marcel Marceau and many more.

On 18 June 1994, the theatre hosted a live showing on a large screen of the Ireland v Italy soccer World Cup, which Ireland won 1–0. All seats were taken by cheering fans and bewildered tourists joined in as conga lines formed in the aisles of the Olympia to celebrate the defeat of a team that had put Ireland out of the previous World Cup. It was all theatre.

DUBLIN CASTLE

Dublin Castle isn't really a castle at all, but people referred to it as such in recognition of its place of power in Irish affairs. Nowadays, it houses the revenue commissioners, an art gallery, headquarters of the drugs squad and State apartments. It was home for many years to an official tribunal enquiry into planning matters that rambled on for a very long time and cost millions to pursue.

The site of Dublin Castle dates back to King John in the early thirteenth century, who was the first, but not the last, British monarch to also claim to be King of Ireland. A claim the Irish thought risible.

The castle served as a royal residence, being the town apartments of the Viceroy, who ruled Ireland on behalf of the reigning monarch. He, for it was always a he, lived in Dublin Castle, which was the centre of society while the Viceroy was in residence. When the Viceroy moved to Phoenix Park for the summer, a distance of a few miles, society centred on the park.

The administration was Protestant, so a Catholic who paid too much obeisance to the rulers there was known pejoratively as a Castle Catholic. Ironically, the last Viceroy of Ireland was Viscount FitzAlan of Derwent, a Catholic who served in the post until independence was achieved in 1922 and the Irish Free State came into being.

GANDON

Built in 1794, O'Connell Bridge was originally called Carlisle Bridge (named after Viceroy Frederick Howard, 5th Earl of Carlisle) and was designed by architect James Gandon (1743–1823). Its keystone heads, by Edward Smyth, depicted the Liffey and Neptune: the river about to meet the sea. When the bridge was widened and realigned in 1880, the heads of Liffey and Neptune were incorporated into nearby 30–32 Sir John Rogerson's Quay.

Not far downstream is another of Gandon's designs – the 1780s Customs House, and one of the finest buildings in Dublin. This too has stone heads of river gods and the ocean on the keystones of the ground floor arches, likewise created by Edward Smyth. Acknowledging the art of an earlier era, many of these gods appeared on the original Sir John Lavery Irish bank notes of the new Irish Free State.

Gandon was also responsible for designing the Four Courts (built between 1796 and 1802 on the Liffey banks), Custom House, Kings Inns and several other impressive architectural projects in the city. He also designed Abbeville in north county Dublin, which was the final home of a former Taoiseach, Charles Haughey.

For all that he shaped the city, Gandon was not a Dubliner. The grandson of a French Huguenot refugee, Gandon was born at New Bond Street in London. In his adult years, he lived at Lucan in Cannonbrook House, which overlooks the village of Lucan on the banks of the Liffey. He retired to, and died at, Canonbrook on 24 December 1823. His remains are buried in Drumcondra, Dublin.

ÁRAS AN UACHTARÁIN

Áras an Uachtaráin is the home and workplace of the President of Ireland. Situated in Phoenix Park to the west of the city, Park Ranger Nathaniel Clements built the original house for his own use at the end of the eighteenth century. However, in 1767, after a decree was issued stating that the King's representative for Ireland (the Viceroy) should reside in Ireland, the government bought the Lodge for £25,000 from the Clements family as an official residence. In 1778, Lord Carlisle became the first Viceroy to reside in the newly acquired building, which was renamed the Viceregal Lodge.

The original house was a neat, unassuming brick building, with the rooms conveniently disposed, as was the custom of the day. Offices projected on either side and were joined to the house by circular sweeps. Inside, the hall was top lit at the entrance end by a window and a large saloon, with an elaborate compartmented ceiling and floral plaster. It was heated by twin chimney pieces.

In 1802, the Earl of Hardwicke ordered two new wings to be added to the Lodge, and by 1816 a Portland stone portico of four ionic columns had been constructed.

There have been additions made to the house and grounds over the years, the most noteworthy being the establishment of formal gardens by Decimus Burton in the 1840s, an addition of the East Wing in 1849 for the State visit of Queen Victoria, installation of mains gas supply in 1852 and electricity in 1908, and the extension of the West Wing for the visit of King George V in 1911.

The present occupier is the ninth President of Ireland, Michael Higgins, TD.

BLACK JACK

Many motorists pass over the Blackquiere Bridge in Phibsboro, Dublin without realising the provenance of the name. The bridge was named after Black Jack John Blaquiere, a politician of French Huguenot descent, who served as Chief Secretary for Ireland between 1772 and 1777; a job that was, in effect, deputy leader to the Viceroy. In addition to his duties as Chief Secretary, Blaquiere was named Bailiff of Phoenix Park.

As bailiff he received a four-roomed cottage at what is now Deerfield, the US Ambassador's residence, which he lost no time in extending into a Georgian house on 60 acres. Blaquiere annexed some 30 acres of the park for his new residence, but was later challenged in a Dublin court by Lawyer Napper Tandy – one of the founders of the United Irishmen, who would later rise in armed rebellion in 1798 – over the land grab. Unsurprisingly, the court found in Blaquiere's favour: he was, after all, number two in power in Ireland at the time. However, while the court found in his favour on the land snatch, it delivered a ruling on use of the park by everyone else. The court stated: 'It was only by leave of the King the citizens had liberty to recreate themselves (in the park) under restrictions such as not riding on cars, not bringing in dogs or guns, and not sending their servants to air their horses during the fencing month.'

The new house was finished in 1776, and in 1782 the government bought it as an official residence for the Chief Secretary of Ireland for £7,000. But it was not all stately aplomb in the park from then on. In Phoenix Park on a Sunday at that time, up to 300 tents could be pitched on the adjoining Fifteen Acres for the sale of whiskey and for gambling. Such shenanigans went on under the rule of Black Jack Sir John. In addition to drunken debauchery, the grasslands were overgrazed, and the roads left unrepaired, it was charged. Not surprisingly, Blaquiere was bought out of the job by the government of the day.

HUGUENOTS AND WEAVERS

For a small group of immigrants to Ireland in the seventeenth century, the Huguenots left many traces of their passing. They were members of the Protestant Reformed Church of France, who fled the country following religious persecution against them.

Their graveyard lies beside the Shelbourne Hotel on present-day Merrion Row.

A large number of Huguenots settled in the Liberties, and, due to them being skilled weavers, the area became known for this industry. In 1815, a Tenter House was erected in Cork Street, financed by Thomas Pleasants. A brick building 275ft long, three stories high and with a central cupola, the Tenter House had central heating, powered by four furnaces, and provided a place for weavers to stretch their material in bad weather.

So many workers took pride in the weaving trade that for years afterwards, and well past the demise of the industry, people still listed their occupation as 'weaver' on official documents.

By then, many weavers had fallen into destitution.

The Iveagh Trust, the Dublin Artisans Dwellings Company and the City Council redeveloped part of the area into affordable housing and parkland in the early to mid-twentieth century, by which time the slums had been wiped away. It is still known as the Tenters by Dubliners.

MARTELLO TOWERS

Martello towers sprang up all over the Irish coastline in the nineteenth century. The early towers were originally built to defend the country from Napoleonic invasion.

Perhaps the best know Martello tower in Ireland is the one at Sandycove in Dublin Bay, where James Joyce stayed for a few days, later immortalising it in his Dublin novel *Ulysses*. Another Martello tower, further along the coast at Seapoint, houses an exhibition on the history of Dublin's Martello towers, offering guided tours that allow access to the roof and its 18lb cannon during the summer months.

Martello towers were two-storey defensive forts, about 12m high and with walls 2½m thick that had narrow slits for defensive musket fire. Entry was by ladder to a door about 3m from the base, above which was a slotted platform that allowed for downward fire on attackers by defenders. The flat roof had a high parapet and a raised platform in the centre, with a pivot for a cannon that would traverse a 360° arc. Ammunition, water, stores and provisions were kept on the ground floor, which served as the magazine and storeroom. Above that, a garrison of twenty-four men and one officer lived on the first floor, which was divided into several rooms and had fireplaces built into the walls for cooking and heating. The officer and men lived in separate rooms of almost equal size, as they should, so they could complain about one another. A cistern within the fort supplied the garrison with water and an internal drainage system, linked to the roof, enabled rainwater to refill the cistern.

All in all a desirable residence, especially since Napoleon did not hove to off the Irish coast at all.

NUMBER 29 GEORGIAN HOUSE MUSEUM

Number 29 on Fitzwilliam Street is Dublin's Georgian House Museum, where visitors can take a guided tour from the basement to the attic, through rooms furnished with original artefacts as they would have been in the years 1790 to 1820. The displays throughout the museum are supplemented by storyboards, offering information on each room.

The house had been built for John Usher, an apothecary, but he leased it to Mrs Olivia Beatty, the widow of a prominent Dublin wine merchant and mother to seven children. Back then, such houses were home to wealthy families and flocks of servants: the servants lived at the top of the houses and enjoyed smaller windows than the nobs down below, who had large windows and lots of light. Windows were graduated in size according to the importance of each floor. Ground-floor windows were always the largest because they were in the most important quarters, housing the drawing room or dining room. Upper floors were devoted mostly to bedrooms, dressing chambers and private living space where, it was believed, smaller windows were more appropriate.

In Georgian Dublin, houses along the same row were subject to certain conditions so as to maintain the uniform character of the street. Terrace houses were restricted in height to four storeys or less. Number 29 stands across a street intersection from Merrion Square, where, by the end of the eighteenth century, owning a house on Merrion Square was considered essential for social success.

Many Georgian houses were lost to marauding slum landlords in the nineteenth century and rapacious developers in the twentieth.

29 Fitzwilliam Street Lower, Dublin 2 / 01 702 61 65 / www.esb.ie/no29

ABBEY THEATRE

The Abbey Theatre – Ireland's National Theatre – was founded by Nobel Laureate, William Butler Yeats, and Lady Augusta Gregory in 1904. With patronage from Miss Annie Horniman, premises were purchased on Old Abbey Street and on 27 December 1904, the Abbey Theatre opened its doors for the first time.

In 1925, the theatre was awarded an annual subsidy by the new Free State and the Abbey became the first ever State-subsidised theatre in the English-speaking world. In its early years, the theatre was closely associated with the writers of the Irish Literary Revival, many of whom were involved in its founding and most of whom had plays staged there. Many who were associated with the Abbey were also involved in the campaign for national independence, which added frission to its productions.

In 1951, the original buildings of the theatre were damaged by fire and so the company relocated to the Queen's Theatre across the river on Pearse Street. Fifteen years later, to the day, on 18 July 1966 – the year of the 50th anniversary of the Easter Rebellion – the Abbey moved back to its current home, on the same site as before, in a new building designed by Irish architect Michael Scott.

By the early years of the new century and its centenary in 2004, several new locations for the theatre were being proposed for its redevelopment. However, in September 2012, it was announced that the Abbey Theatre had purchased a nearby building on Eden Quay and that a new development would be built on the current site.

26 Lower Abbey Street, Dublin 1 / 01 8787222 / www.abbeytheatre.ie

AMBASSADOR THEATRE

The Ambassador Cinema was Dublin's longest-running cinema until its closure in 1999. The building was constructed as part of the Rotunda Hospital in 1764, as an assembly hall and social rooms on what is now Parnell Square. From 1897 onwards, the venue was given the name Rotund Room, also known as the Rotunda, and it hosted a number of 'moving picture' screenings, which were a great novelty at the time. From about 1908 onwards, it was used more regularly to show film presentations, and in 1910 it became a full-time cinema – in a time when the city centre population was larger than it was to be at the turn of the twenty-first century, the cinema-going public thronged to the venue.

Moving pictures apart, the Rotunda hosted the public launch of the Irish Volunteer organisation on 25 November 1913. The hall was filled to its 4,000-person capacity, with a further 3,000 spilling onto the grounds outside.

In the 1950s, the cinema was redesigned, increasing its seating capacity and adding a balcony with private boxes to the main hall. It reopened on 23 September 1954 as the Ambassador.

On 27 September 1999, after forty-five years, the cinema closed down, due to falling attendances. It is now a music venue and exhibition centre, recently most notable for a travelling display of dead human bodies from China.

Upper O'Connell Street, Dublin 1 / 01 8734344 / www.ambassadortheater.com

THE SPIRE OF DUBLIN

The high, sharp, stainless-steel monument that stands in the middle of O'Connell Street has a number of names. Officially, it is called the Monument of Light, but more colloquially it is known as the Spire of Dublin, or the Spire, and Dubliners have named it the Stiletto in the Ghetto.

The spire stands across from the historic General Post Office (GPO) at 120m in height, 3m in diameter at the base, and some 15cm in diameter at its apex – the sharp bit at the top. It has been classified as the world's tallest sculpture.

The Spire stands where Nelson's Pillar once stood before it was attacked with explosives in 1966. Twice. The first time it was blown apart by the IRA in the 50th anniversary year of the 1916 Rising, and shortly thereafter it was levelled by the Irish Army while removing the stump in time for the 1916 Easter commemorations at the GPO.

Nonetheless, however many were involved in blowing up Nelson's Pillar, lots of minds were involved in the construction of the Spire, which was delayed because of difficulty in obtaining planning permission and environmental regulations. The construction contract was awarded to SIAC-Radley JV. The spire was manufactured by Radley Engineering of Dungarvan, County Waterford and erected by SIAC Construction Ltd. Ian Ritchie Architects, who won a design competition that landed them the project, designed it.

The Spire is constructed from eight hollow tubes of stainless steel and features a tuned mass damper, designed by engineers Arup, to counteract sway. There are lights on top of it to warn passing birds and aeroplanes full of people not to bump into it. The first section was installed on 18 December 2002. Five additional 20m sections were added, with the last one installed on 21 January 2003. It has been there ever since. Thus far.

QUIET PLEASE

Measures to restrict noise levels in the public spaces of Dublin, to ensure they remained a tranquil escape from the hustle and bustle of city life, were announced in 2013. The locations would also be monitored for encroaching sounds from road traffic, trains, aircraft and construction by officials, said the authorities, with conviction.

However, not all places were to be silenced, for that would be asking a lot. The Blessington Basin at Blessington Street and the Cabbage Gardens at Cathedral Lane were the only two parks in central Dublin designated as quiet areas. At least to begin with. Others around the city, in the suburbs if you like, included Edenmore Park and St Anne's Park in Raheny, Mount Bernard Park in Phibsborough, Palmerston Park in Rathmines and Ranelagh Gardens, in Ranelagh. And King Canute-like it was decreed that Dollymount Strand would also become a quieter area than it had been before.

The environment minister, Phil Hogan TD, approved the listed parks for protection against increased levels of environmental noise after a request to him by Dublin City Council to issue a decree. The minister said, in a statement: 'Noise is an unwanted disturbance that negatively impacts on quality of life and may have a detrimental effect on peoples' health and well-being. For this reason it is important that our green spaces and sea frontage are preserved and safeguarded from environmental noise.' Which may or may not include ensuring incoming waves land ashore in a seemly and quiet manner.

According to the council's report, some 23½ per cent of Dubliners live with night-time noise levels, which are classed as undesirable. Therefore, noise limits of 55 decibels during the day and 45 decibels at night would be enforced at the eight new designated quiet areas. Good news for those that don't sleep well.

MOVING STATUES

In the 1980s, during a long damp summer, Marian statues were reported all over Ireland as moving. The phenomenon caused people to fall to their knees to pray, but once the weather improved, the statues remained tranquil, and have done so ever since, with not a move out of any of them – that anybody has noticed.

In the second decade of the twenty-first century, Dublin City Council announced that it was about to make statues move once again in the capital city – all because two lines of light rail were not linked to one another when they were laid down in 2001. Therefore, the Luas Cross City Line needed to link the lines to one another, but in order to do this, cityscape statues had to be moved first.

Molly Malone on Grafton Street was one such statue that was in the way and was to be moved to outside the tourist office in the former St Andrew's church on nearby Suffolk Street. The horse trough on St Stephen's Green, also known to some as the Lady Grattan fountain, was to go into storage. So too was the Steine sculpture, or long stone, at the corner of D'Olier Street and Pearse Street, which was erected in 1986 to commemorate the Viking landings nearby. Though whether those who approved its erection were descended from Vikings was never revealed. The Statue to poet and songwriter Thomas Moore was to be moved from College Green, where it stood over public urinals (now long-closed). James Joyce called this confluence of history and nature the 'Meeting of the Waters', after Moore's melody of the same name.

A spokeswoman for the Luas link-up project said the statues and monuments would be returned to their original locations, or as close as possible to them. Which was good news for fans of these monuments, of which there may be many, or few. We just do not know everything.

9

TRANSPORT, WORK AND COMMERCE

SMITHFIELD MARKET

Smithfield Market has been in existence for one reason or another since at least the tenth century. By 1541, a formal marketplace for cattle was established at Oxmantown Green, to the west of Smithfield, and in 1664, the City Assembly divided Smithfield, Hay Market and Queen Street into ninety-six plots of land to be disposed of by lottery. Some years later, in 1675, John Odacia Formica established the first flint crystal glasshouse on Haymarket. He exported high-quality glassware to the New World, where some of it may be to this day.

By 1879, the buildings at the southern end of Smithfield were demolished to increase the size of the marketplace. However, the market closed in 1883 on an outbreak of foot and mouth disease and was to remain closed for several years. The outbreak resulted in Smithfield being paved in setts.

By the twentieth century, the sale of livestock had moved to the Cattle Market on nearby North Circular Road, although a horse fair continued to be held in Smithfield every month of the year, until a bylaw passed on 14 January 2013 reduced its incidence to twice a year.

Smithfield did not change much over the years in appearance; it remained a large, open space beside the busy city centre. In 1965, the huge, cobbled square was used as Checkpoint Charley in Martin Ritt's adaptation of John Le Carre's *The Spy who Came in from the Cold*, starring Richard Burton. Burton and his wife, Elizabeth Taylor, stayed in the Gresham Hotel on O'Connell Street, causing great excitement at the glamour of it all in the Swinging Sixties.

In 1997, an international design competition for the redevelopment of Smithfield Civic Plaza was won by McGarry Ní Eanaigh Architects and in 2000, Smithfield was the venue chosen to confer the freedom of the city of Dublin on members of Dublin band U2 and on human rights campaigner Aung San Sun Kyi from Burma.

DUBLIN LOCKOUT

Few industrial disputes have had an impact on the consciousness of Dublin as the 1913 Dublin Lockout did. The Lockout was a major industrial dispute that raged between 300 organised employers and some 20,000 workers in the capital between August 1913 and January 1914, provoked by demands for better labour conditions by workers on the one side and resistance to the organisation of the workers into unions by employers on the other.

The Lockout began at 10 a.m. on 26 August 1913, when all trams came to stop on O'Connell Street, with workers seeking pay rises ranging from 1s to 2s a week.

William Martin Murphy, the leader of the employers and owner of the Dublin Tramway Company, locked out members of the Irish Transport and General Workers Union (ITGWU) who refused to sign a pledge to leave the union, which led James Larkin, leader of the ITGWU, to call a general strike. In the disputes that followed more than 20,000 workers were either locked out of their jobs by their employers or went on strike. By the end of August, the city was in a state of unrest, with riots in Ringsend, Beresford Place and Eden Quay, and O'Connell Street, during which the police baton-charged crowds of protestors, causing injuries and fatalities. In response, the Citizen Army was formed as a militia, armed with hurleys, to defend the strikers.

The Lockout continued for six fractious months. By early 1914, many of the workers were driven back to work through hunger and want, but the union they formed remained in existence and the armed and militant Citizen Army was later to fight in the Easter Rebellion, which began in Dublin on Easter Monday 1916.

HANSFIELD STATION: MORE TRAINS THAN PEOPLE ON THE FIRST DAY

On the day a handsome new railway station opened in West Dublin, more trains arrived at the station than did intending passengers. The €10 million railway station in West Dublin opened for business in 2013, more than three years after it was built. Originally designed as a piece of infrastructure to enhance the commuting experience of local residents, the station and its service was a victim of the economic collapse following the Celtic Tiger years.

Hansfield Station in Ongar, Dublin 15, was built on the Dublin to M3 Parkway rail line in 2010, but could not be used because an access road to it had not been completed, leaving it landlocked. The developer that built the station had been unable to complete the road because of its financial difficulties. However, after agreement was reached between Fingal County Council, the National Transport Authority and Irish Rail, the road was finished. While it awaited a resolution, trains passed by on the rail line to other places but did not stop at the silent station.

When the station finally opened, local politicians turned out for the official opening, only to find that most people had either forgotten there was a station there, or had made alternative arrangements for travelling.

HELLO DUBLIN CALLING

A new phone line for Dublin was announced in May 1913 – this was big news in the second decade of the twentieth century. Since 1852, a submarine telegraph cable had linked Ireland to Britain between Howth and Holyhead, but the arrival of a phone line would mean voice could be carried as well. A new telephone cable was being laid under the Irish Sea to give Dublin a direct connection with the English telephone system for the first time, and businessmen in Dublin warmly welcomed the announcement from the House of Commons, in London, that the cable would be operational within three months.

The first telephone exchange in Ireland was opened in 1880 by the United Telephone Company on the top floor of Commercial Buildings in Dame Street. It had five subscribers, but none had direct links from one to another; instead, callers had to go through an operator to be connected to another subscriber. Moreover, no service was available outside of the hours of 9 a.m. to midnight and telephone circuits were confined to local areas, with contact between cities and countries requiring a call being put through a trunk system of exchanges. Trunk routes ran alongside the railways because the Post Office had free wayleave rights along the route under agreements with the Irish railway companies. Twenty years later, by 1900, there were fifty-six exchanges working in Ireland.

Making a call was a complicated business. Anyone in Dublin wishing to speak to another person in London had to have the call passed through a series of connections from Dublin to Belfast, from there under the Irish Sea to Glasgow or Carlisle, and then down length of Britain to London. However, because these lines were also being used by towns and cities en route through England, calls from far away in Dublin had to wait in turn to be connected. Such calls often took many hours to be put through; time, perhaps, for reflection before speaking – not always a bad idea.

PROPERTY INVESTMENT

Dublin's early twentieth-century tenements were investment properties that would be described as buy-to-let investments in the modern climate. At least, they were from the point-of-view of the owners. Many people made their money from rents collected from tenants, and such incomes were often shared as gifts with others: a bride's dowry could be the collective rent of two houses filled with people.

One hundred years ago, almost a quarter of Dubliners lived in one-room flats that were, for the most part, concentrated in the area inside the ring of canals north and south of the city. Not many new builds took place in the nineteenth century within the canals, following the closure of the Irish Parliament and the transfer of society and influence to London.

However, in the following century, at a time of poverty and famine, poor, rural people moved to the city, swelling the population. The well-to-do who remained moved to the suburbs beyond the canals to Rathmines and Drumcondra and Inchicore, many of whom were influenced in their choice of destination by the new tram lines emanating from the city centre. Housing was in demand, and, as time passed and prosperity diminished, the old Georgian houses that had originally been built for just one family at a time and its servants began to accommodate many more. Large family rooms were sub-divided into smaller units, each housing a family of its own, and some of the houses had so many one-family rooms occupied that they were like small towns in themselves; the shared hallway being the main street.

Landlords carried out little or no maintenance to the structure of the houses and, as a result, the condition of houses declined. Indeed, on 2 September 1913, numbers 66 and 67 Church Street suddenly collapsed into the street, taking their occupants with them. They tumbled down at 9 p.m. when darkness had fallen, making the event even more traumatic for those involved. A pall of smoke and dust lay over all for twenty-four hours afterwards, making it hard to see who was dead or injured and who could be rescued. The situation was unchanged even in daylight. Rescue efforts were hampered by a lack of certainty about how many were inside the buildings when they came down. Seven were killed in the incident and their funerals brought the city to a standstill. Elsewhere, an official enquiry found that, in one place, thirty-six people were living and cooking on an open fire in a room measuring 32ft × 13ft.

Rents varied according to the space occupied, and occupants of the garrets were often said to be living under the slates. The following weekly rents were typical in 1913 when the houses in Church Street collapsed:

Front kitchen 2*s*
Back kitchen 1*s* 6*d*
Front parlour 3*s* 6*d*
Back dining room 3*s*
Upstairs 3*s*
Garrets 2*s* to 2*s* 6*d*

GUINNESS BARGES

The old Dublin myth that Guinness is brewed using the water from the River Liffey is false; nevertheless, the brewery did use the Liffey for many years as a means of transport for its kegged products. They were loaded onto barges and sailed down the river to where Guinness ships were moored beside the Customs House to take the barrels away to export markets. By the second half of the twentieth century, the company owned two full-sized tankers – *Lady Patricia* and *Miranda Guinness* – dedicated to exporting stout in bulk from a jetty close to where the Talbot Memorial Bridge is today. As road transport methods improved, however, the use of barges on the Liffey faded, finally ending on Midsummer Day, 1961. Product, thereafter, was driven down the city quays in stainless-steel trailers hauled by trucks.

In earlier times, steam-driven Guinness barges were a daily sight on the river when the first purpose-built jetty at St James Quay, outside the brewery's dispatch yard, was opened in 1873. A narrow-gauge railway brought barrels from the brewery to the jetty and then the barges puffed away downstream, according to the tide and clearance beneath the city bridges – smoke stacks were hinged to lie flat when clearance was doubtful. The barges were named after Irish rivers and Dublin place names; in fact, it was a Dublin pastime to challenge someone to name all barges in the fleet. Later additions to the fleet could reach speeds of 7½ knots with a full load of 105 tons aboard.

DUBLIN BIKES

Dublin is a relatively flat city that is easy to cycle about in. In the mid-twentieth century shoals of bikes poured along the streets as people pedalled to work or study, or the cinema in the evening. So widespread was the use of bicycles that anyone caught riding a bike without a light, once the official daily lighting-up time had passed, would see the inside of a courtroom on charges. Being drunk in charge of a bicycle was another offence not unheard of in the city courts.

However, cycling waned as motor transport became more popular, although development of dedicated cycle lanes in recent years has allowed more cyclists to take to the streets once more, in safety. Dublin City Council and advertising company JCDecaux even agreed a scheme, in 2009, whereby the company would provide bicycles and maintain them in return for advertising space on seventy-two advertising panels on the city streets. The company provided 450 bicycles at forty pick-up and drop-off stations in various locations – users simply pick up a bike at one place and return it to a station beside their destination.

By 2013, so popular had the service become that a €35 million deal was announced to expand the scheme, with 950 new bicycles and fifty-eight additional hire points being provided. The new contract did not involve additional advertising sites; instead, the council would pay the company €1.925 million a year for ten years to run the service.

TRANSPORT MUSEUM

Much of what once filled the streets of Dublin with traffic may still be seen in a quiet place on the slope of the Hill of Howth in a northern suburb of Dublin. The Transport Museum, located in the Heritage Depot, contains items dating from 1883 up until 1984, featuring buses, lorries, trucks, fire engines, trams and tractors. Also exhibited is the restored Hill of Howth No. 9 Tram.

The Transport Museum Society of Ireland began with a 1949 effort to preserve three Dublin trams. Totally voluntary, the society became a limited company in 1971 and is now a registered charity, operating to international museum standards. Begun modestly, as funds and opportunity allowed, the collection increased at an annual rate of five units in the early years of the present century. It now totals 170 vehicles with an average age of forty-six years. The museum is funded by a minimal entry fee, unlike The National Museum, National Gallery and National History museums, which are funded by government.

Film companies use vehicles from the museum to fill the streets of Dublin when shooting period films and during St Patrick's Festival each year, a Leyland bus from the collection becomes a static story bus parked on Merrion Square. Here, children can once more sit on the seats and take a journey through the imagination on a bus once used by their ancestors to get to school and other places of enjoyment.

AN POST

The headquarters of An Post, the Irish postal service, is the General Post Office on O'Connell Street, where a statue of Cúchulainn – a slain Irish mythological hero – marks the spot where the Proclamation of Independence was read out on Easter Monday, declaring autonomy in its affairs for Ireland.

Every working day, 10,000 rural, urban, full-time and part-time postal staff collect, process and deliver more than 2.5 million items of mail to 2.1 million business and residential addresses, using a road fleet of 2,778 vehicles and 1,645 bicycles. They serve 1.7 million customers every week through the national network of more than 1,100 post offices and 175 postal agents.

In 2013, An Post issued three commemorative stamps to commemorate the 1913 Lockout labour dispute.

An Post reminds us that the letter was the only way people could communicate over distance before telephones, email and social networking were developed, helping families keep in touch, merchants and traders to carry out their business, and government to communicate with its representatives throughout the country.

Its headquarters, the GPO, was opened in January 1818, at a build cost of £50,000. Francis Johnston, an architect with the Board of Works, designed the building in Greek revival style. The main section is made with Wicklow granite and the portico, the roof structure over the entrance, is made from Portland stone.

During the 1916 Rising, the GPO was one of three Dublin landmarks – the Four Courts and the Custom House being the others – to be destroyed in the fighting. The GPO was rebuilt and reopened in 1929. The new national radio station, then called 2RN, moved from its single studio in Little Denmark Street, in 1928, and into new headquarters in the General Post Office. It is now out in Donnybrook, trading as RTÉ. The GPO is still where it was and functions as a post office and poste restante for travellers.

DUBLIN SHIPBUILDING

For nearly two centuries Dublin had a vibrant shipbuilding industry. The *Ouzel Galley*, which disappeared for a number of years before returning to its home port of Dublin, is reputed to have been built in the late seventeenth century somewhere along where Townsend Street now runs, just a few hundred metres from O'Connell Bridge. In those days all that was needed to build and launch a new ship was a sloping bank and sufficient depth of water in which to float the new boat. That and an open space to store the timber and a saw-pit to cut it to shape, together with a hut for standing in out of the rain on bad days and for storing whatever rudimentary documentation was required for the current project.

Dublin has the distinction of having constructed the first catamarans in the western world, and, according to maritime historian Pat Sweeney, they were designed by Sir William Petty. Petty's creation, the *Invention*, was built on the banks of the Liffey and launched in 1662 – the same year that Smock Alley Theatre began its royal life further upstream, though the events are unconnected, as far as we know. In a sailing race on 6 January 1663, three other boats were easily beaten by the *Invention*, which reached a speed of 16 knots in a challenge race, it was reported.

By 1968, the government of the day said in the Dáil that for economic reasons connected with intense competition, the building of new ships had been discontinued for some time in Dublin. The reduction in the number of Irish-owned ships using the Port of Dublin, seriously reduced the volume of ship-repair work available, in turn, leading to a fading away of ship work in Dublin, for now.

POINT DEPOT

The Point Theatre is located at the point of Dublin's North Wall Quay of the River Liffey, before the docks area poured itself further into the sea in an extension to the port, hence the name. Constructed in 1878, the building was originally a train depot to serve the busy port, but ceased operations in the 1980s.

In the late 1980s, developers fitted out the venue with balconies, offices and backstage facilities. Before the fit-out was completed, U2 recorded 'Van Diemen's Land' for their 1988 album *Rattle and Hum*.

From 1988 to 2007, the building was used as an events venue and has functioned as an ice rink, a boxing arena, a conference hall, an exhibition centre, a wrestling ring, a theatre, an opera house and a three-ring circus. It hosted the Eurovision Song Contest on three separate occasions in the 1990s, as well as the 1999 MTV European Music Awards. Furthermore, the Point was the venue that introduced Riverdance to the world as an interval act during the 1994 Eurovision Song Contest, and Westlife performed at the venue for a record breaking thirteen consecutive nights in 2001 on their 'Where Dreams Come True' tour. The final event before its closure and rebranding was a boxing card featuring local boxer Bernard Dunne on 25 August 2007. The Point closed in the summer of 2007 for major redevelopment and emerged a year later, in July 2008, as the O2.

CANALS

Dublin city is traditionally defined as that area lying between two canals: the Royal and the Grand, the southernmost of the pair of canals that connect Dublin with the River Shannon in the west.

Proposals for connecting Dublin to the Shannon were voiced as early as 1715, but it was some time later, in 1757, when the Irish Parliament granted Thomas Omer £20,000 to start construction of a canal. Two years later, 13km of canal were completed towards Dublin from the River Liffey, near Sallins in neighbouring County Kildare. A twice-weekly passenger service from Sallins to Dublin started in 1780, which was horse-drawn and took a while to arrive, as might be imagined.

The Royal Canal, on the north side, was originally built for freight and passenger transportation from the River Liffey at Dublin to Longford. The canal fell into disrepair in the late twentieth century, but much of the waterway was restored for navigation. The canal to the River Shannon was reopened on 1 October 2010 and includes a high bridge over the M50 motorway, where the canal in the sky and its traffic overflies road traffic below. At the Dublin end, the canal reaches the Liffey through a sequence of dock and locks at Spencer Dock, at the modern Financial Services Centre, with a final sea lock to manage access to the river and sea.

At one time, city carters were paid extra to deliver goods beyond the canals from the city centre or docks area. The last working cargo barge passed through the Grand Canal in 1960.

Brendan Behan immortalised the banks of the Royal Canal in 'The Ould Triangle', his famous Dublin ballad about life in Mountjoy Gaol, situated beside the canal.

SUNLIGHT CHAMBERS

Sunlight Chambers at Capel Street Bridge on the corner of Parliament Street and Essex Quay was built in 1902 as the Dublin offices for Lord Lever of Lever Brothers (the English soap and detergent manufacturers), hence the building's name, which was derived from one of the company's products, Sunlight soap. Sunlight Chambers was designed by the Liverpool architect Edward Ould, who also designed Lever's model village, Port Sunlight, for Merseyside factory workers. It was built in a romantic, Italianate style, with wide, overhanging eaves, tiled roof and arcaded upper floors. On its completion, the *Irish Builder* called it the ugliest building in Dublin, which may have been due to the fact that a foreign architect had been hired and not a local lad, or maybe not; beauty or ugliness is often in the eye of the beholder.

Nonetheless, the building boasts one of the most unusual building features in Dublin: two multi-coloured, terracotta friezes, designed by Conrad Dressler, depicting the history of hygiene and Lever's part in it. They show people working at making and using soap – the extraction of raw materials to manufacture soap, the bargaining of merchants buying oils and scents and women scrubbing and washing clothes. Ironically, in recent years, with airborne pollution, the friezes became faded under layers of dirt before a restoration project restored the building to its multi-coloured brilliance. Whether they caused people to rush out and buy Sunlight soap is neither here nor there, anymore. They are simply a part of Dublin now.

10

BATTLES
AND WARS

BRIAN BORU

In the eleventh century, with a population of fewer than 500,000 people, Ireland had more than 150 kings, with greater or lesser domains lording it over everyone; Brian Boru wanted to be boss of them all and be called the High King.

They say he crossed the Liffey on foot at Islandbridge in 1014 on his way to the Battle of Clontarf with the Norsemen because the bridge had not yet been built and he could not wait. At Clontarf on Good Friday, Boru's armies confronted the armies of Leinster and Dublin under Máel Morda. The resulting Battle of Clontarf was a bloody affair, with Brian and his son, Murchad, among those killed, which was not what Brian had planned, at all. His opponents were Norsemen, both the Norse-Gaels of Dublin and the Norsemen from neighbouring countries. And so, although the leader was killed, the battle was duly reported by Irish historians as being the routing of the Danes by the Good Brian – the Irishman who wanted to unite his countrymen under his flag.

There are many legends concerning how Boru was killed, from dying in heroic man-to-man combat to being killed by the fleeing Viking mercenary Brodir while praying in his tent at Clontarf, it being Good Friday. Whatever way he perished, Boru was dead and that was that.

After his death, Boru's body was taken to Swords in County Dublin to be waked and then on to Armagh to be buried. His tomb is said to be in the north wall of St Patrick's Cathedral in the city of Armagh.

CULLENSWOOD MASSACRE

The Normans may have been victorious in their initial invasion campaigns of the twelfth century, but not all the Irish acknowledged defeat (despite lots of people losing their heads to the Normans). Even in their settlements, Norman townspeople continued to be vulnerable to attacks by Irish clans and fear of such violence was ever present. In particular, the O'Byrnes and the O'Tooles made frequent incursions from their strongholds in the Dublin and Wicklow mountains to attack Dublin and environs.

Such marauding led to a 'them and us' mentality among those inside the stockade or Pale surrounding Dublin. Such a siege mentality can be stifling and from time to time the besieged will venture forth, just to show they can. In medieval Dublin this took the form of an annual pilgrimage to the area called Fiodh Chuilinn, the modern-day Cullenswood in Ranelagh. Everything was fine until 1209, when 500 recent settlers from Bristol were massacred by the O'Toole clan during an outing outside the city limits. It was a Monday. Thereafter, every year on the anniversary of Black Monday, Dublin citizens would march out of the city to the spot where the atrocity had happened and raise a black banner in the direction of the mountains to challenge the Irish to battle in a gesture of symbolic defiance.

The Irish accepted the challenge so often and so vigorously that hundreds of years later, even into the seventeenth century, participants in this excursion had to be guarded by the city militia against the mountain enemy. Not so much now.

THE BRUCE

In 1317, when Edward Bruce was marauding around the north of Ireland subjugating anyone he met on behalf of his older brother Robert, he sent an army southwards to attack Dublin. Not wishing to make it easy for Bruce, the citizens of Dublin decided to burn down the suburbs immediately outside the city's fortifications to prevent the Scots using them in the event of siege. A good idea when they planned it, most likely, but one that went so badly wrong that the pressing army went away and left the residents to destroy the city on their own.

And destroy it they did. It was said that Dubliners broke the bridge of Dublin and demolished a number of buildings, using the stone to strengthen the town defences, but it was the out-of-control fire that wreaked the most havoc. The fire was most unusual in that, while it was started intentionally on Thomas Street by the citizens, it soon spread of its own accord and destroyed much of the city. According to eyewitnesses at the time, the church of St John and the Chappell of St Marie Maudlen, together with the monastery St Mary's Abbey and the church of St Patrick (later St Patrick's Cathedral), quickly burnt down.

The Scottish army, which was camped at Castleknock to the west above the Liffey Valley, saw the city ablaze and decided they would leave Dubliners to their own devices and moved on to pillage Kildare, for which Kildare gave no thanks to Dublin.

For a long time after the fire, a householder whose house went up in flames was offered the choice of paying a fine or of being thrown into his own fire for his sins. It made people more careful of playing with fire.

SILKEN THOMAS

In the sixteenth century, Anglo-Irish strong men held power beyond the Pale surrounding Dublin, but in the neighbouring county of Kildare, it was Garret Mór Fitzgerald who ruled. Fitzgerald was Earl of Kildare and a powerful Lord Deputy who held court at his stronghold at Maynooth Castle, until his death in 1513.

When Henry VIII summoned Fitzgerald's son, Garret Óg (Silken Thomas' brother), to London in 1533, false rumours spread that Garret had been executed in the Tower of London. Hearing this, the twenty-one-year-old Silken Thomas (so-called for the silk worn on his followers' helmets) reacted swiftly and rode through Dublin with a large band of followers on 11 June 1534, flinging down his Sword of State. Henry treated it an act of open revolt and confined Garret Óg and his brothers to the Tower, where Garret Óg died some two months later.

By then, Garret Mór Fitzgerald had also died and Silken Thomas inherited his father's position, though this was never recognised by the king. Nonetheless, Thomas's men cut the water supply to Dublin and a siege began.

Thomas's first assault was directed at the main Castle Gate; however, the defences held strong, so he launched a second attack on Ship Street, but his men were forced back by the guns of the fortress. His final attack went as badly wrong as did its two predecessors.

A relief force, under the newly appointed Lord Deputy, William Skeffington, arrived and laid siege to his Kildare stronghold of Maynooth Castle. When the occupants agreed to the terms of surrender, they were put to death; an act that was the start of the fall of the House of Kildare. Thomas was taken to London where he was hanged at Tyburn.

Such treachery on the part of the victors is still remembered as the Pardon of Maynooth.

BATTLE OF RATHMINES

Looking at the prosperous suburb with modern eyes, the Battle of Rathmines may sound like a local skirmish, but its outcome paved the way for Oliver Cromwell to run riot across the country to his everlasting infamy. The battle was fought in August 1649 between an English Parliamentarian army under Michael Jones, which held Dublin, and an army composed of Irish Confederate and English Royalist troops under the command of the serving Viceroy: the Earl of Ormonde, James Butler.

In July, Ormonde marched his force of 11,000 men to the outskirts of Dublin where he took Rathfarnham Castle and camped at Palmerston Park in Rathgar, about 4km south of the city. The battle ended in the rout of the Confederate/Royalist army. The pursuing Roundheads cut down the fleeing Royalist and Confederate soldiers; Ormonde also lost his entire artillery train and all his baggage and supplies. In the aftermath of the battle, Ormonde withdrew his remaining troops from around Dublin, allowing Oliver Cromwell and the New Model Army to land at Ringsend with 15,000 veteran troops on 15 August.

One unintended consequence of the action was the wandering of a wounded horse into a tavern where the modern Upper Camden Street runs. The place became known as The Bleeding Horse public house, a name still carried to this day, showing that while Dubliners respect history they never forget a horse that likes a drink.

ROBERT EMMET

Robert Emmet – a member of the executive of the revolutionary United Irishmen – led a brief rebellion on 23 July 1803, leading ninety rebels on an abortive attack of Dublin Castle to establish a provisional government. On their way through the Liberties they came upon the carriage of the Lord Chief Justice Kilwarden and dragged him out and killed him. His daughter raised the alarm at the castle and the rebels dispersed. Emmet was later captured and found guilty of treason.

So far, so little, but the Irish are great with words and Emmet made a speech from the dock that lived after him and was used as inspiration by succeeding generations of revolutionaries:

My Lords:
What have I to say why sentence of death should not be pronounced on me according to law? I have nothing to say that can alter your predetermination, nor that it will become me to say with any view to the mitigation of that sentence which you are here to pronounce, and I must abide by.

He concluded with:

I have but one request to ask at my departure from this world – it is the charity of its silence! Let no man write my epitaph: for as no man who knows my motives dare now vindicate them. Let not prejudice or ignorance asperse them. Let them and me repose in obscurity and peace, and my tomb remain uninscribed, until other times, and other men, can do justice to my character; when my country takes her place among the nations of the earth, then, and not till then, let my epitaph be written. I have done.

Emmet was hung, drawn and quartered outside St Catherine's church, Thomas Street, on 20 September 1803. To this day, it is not known where his body is buried.

BATTLE OF TALLAGHT, 5 MARCH 1867

The Battle of Tallaght was not even a fight, according to local historian Malachi Horan, who reported that the Fenians took their stand before Tallaght Barracks on Main Street without a plan or a leader or any hope of either, having known some of the rebels himself in later years.

The old constabulary barracks on Main Street was the scene of the main engagement, which occurred during the Fenian rising on 5 March 1867. At midnight, the Fenians had moved out to assemble on Tallaght Hill, but the large number of armed men passing along the road to the gathering place alarmed the police in Tallaght, who then sent warning to the nearest barracks.

There was said to be some 5,000 Fenians there that night, but no leaders showed up, for some reason, causing confusion among the would-be revolutionaries as to what to do next. As a result, they did not cause much trouble for the police, and head constable Burke ordered his fourteen men to fire on them as they arrived on Main Street. One was killed and some more wounded. That was the battle. There were other incidents as the night progressed, but no major engagement.

However, what happened afterwards, as the rebels scattered in flight, has been remembered more than the battle itself. The Scots Greys, a hard bunch of men, based in Portobello Barracks, followed on. Some of the defeated were killed, some eighty-three were captured in the immediate aftermath and sixty-five were later arrested. Some were given twenty years' exile in Australia for little more than a shouting match.

DUBLIN FUSILIERS

The Royal Dublin Fusiliers was an infantry regiment of the British Army created in 1881. It was one of eight Irish regiments raised and garrisoned in Ireland, with its home depot in Naas, County Kildare.

They fought in the Second Boer War (1899-1900) and Fusiliers' Arch, a memorial to those who died in the action, was erected at St Stephen's Green in 1907, funded by public subscription. Inscribed on the memorial are the names of the 212 Fusiliers who lost their lives in the war. Nationalists promptly named the memorial 'Traitor's

Gate', a nickname it carries to this day. Nonetheless, the arch remains one of the few colonialist monuments in Dublin not blown up in Ireland's post-independence history.

During the First World War, a further six battalions were raised and the Fusiliers saw action on the Western Front, the Mediterranean and the Middle East. In the course of that war three Victoria Crosses were awarded. Many of those killed while on service with the regiment and some of their relatives are buried in the Grangegorman Military Cemetery beside Phoenix Park.

Three battalions of the Royal Dublin Fusiliers attacked rebels in the Easter Rising of 1916 in Dublin, which resulted in eleven of the Royal Dublin Fusiliers being killed and thirty-five more wounded. On Irish independence in 1922, the British Army disbanded six of a total of thirteen Irish regiments, including the Royal Dublin Fusiliers. Thousands of former British soldiers and Dublin Fusiliers joined the Free State government's newly formed National Army.

THE 1916 EASTER RISING

The Easter Rising, also know as the Easter Rebellion, was an armed insurrection staged during Easter Week in 1916 in an attempt to end British rule. Most of the military action took place in Dublin after countermanding orders had been issued by Volunteer Chief of Staff Eoin MacNeill on the previous day to units of armed Volunteers around the country not to turn out for manoeuvres, which he had discovered were a cover for nationwide organised insurrection.

Organised by seven members of the Military Council of the Irish Republican Brotherhood, a secret organisation within the Irish Volunteers, the Rising began on 24 April 1916 and lasted for six days. Members of the Irish Volunteers, joined by the Irish Citizen Army and 200 members of Cumann na mBan, seized key locations in Dublin, including the GPO, and proclaimed the Irish Republic. The Rising was suppressed after six days of fighting and its leaders were court-martialled and executed in Kilmainham Gaol.

While the rising failed in its objective, its leaders succeeded in bringing physical force republicanism back to the forefront of Irish politics, in fact, their deaths swung public opinion in their favour.

Support grew so much for independence that in December 1918, republicans, by then represented by the Sinn Féin party, won seventy-three Irish seats out of 105 in the General Election to the British Parliament. They refused to sit in Westminster and instead convened the First Dáil in the Mansion House in Dublin and declared the independence of the Irish Republic.

The action amounted to a declaration of war and led on through the War of Independence to the Treaty with the British in 1922, when twenty-six counties became the Irish Free State and six north-eastern counties remained within the United Kingdom of Great Britain and Northern Ireland. Where they remain to this day.

THE BATTLE OF DUBLIN

Not everyone who had fought in the Irish War of Independence agreed on the terms of the treaty with the British, and so a civil war began in 1922.

On 14 April 1922, about 200 anti-treaty IRA militants, led by Rory O'Connor, occupied the Four Courts in Dublin.

The Battle of Dublin is an overall title given to a week of street battles from 28 June to 5 July 1922 that marked the beginning of the Irish Civil War. The fighting began with an assault by Provisional Government forces on the Four Courts building, which had been occupied by the Anti-Treaty IRA. It ended in a decisive victory for the Provisional Government.

Michael Collins, leading the government forces, accepted a British offer of artillery loaned by Winston Churchill for use by the new Irish Army.

Two 18lb field guns were placed on Parliament Street and Winetavern Street, across the Liffey from the Four Courts complex, and after a final ultimatum they began their bombardment on the 28 June.

The garrison consisted of roughly 180 men drawn from the 1st and 2nd Battalions of the IRA's 1st Dublin Brigade, armed for the most part only with rifles, five Thompson sub-machine guns and light machine guns and a captured armoured car. The shelling caused the historic Four Courts to catch fire. The Irish Public Record Office located in the Four Courts, which had been used as an ammunition store, was wrecked by a huge explosion, destroying thousands of Irish state and religious archives.

DUBLIN BOMBINGS

The northern Troubles spilled onto the streets of Dublin on 17 May 1974 with the Dublin and Monaghan bombings, in which four bombs were detonated. Three of the bombs were car bombs that went off in Dublin on a Friday evening as people made their way home from work in the middle of a bus strike.

No warnings were given before the bombs exploded, the first of which went off at 5.30 p.m. on Parnell Street, where ten people were killed, including two infant girls and their parents. The second bomb, on nearby Talbot Street, killed twelve people outright, with a further two deaths occurring in the days following. Thirteen of the fourteen dead were women, including one who was nine months pregnant. The final Dublin bomb exploded minutes later across the river on South Leinster Street, near to Trinity College, where two women died on the street. Ninety minutes later, a fourth bomb exploded in Monaghan, killing seven.

The attacks killed thirty-three civilians and wounded almost 300 – the highest number of casualties in any one day during the Troubles. Most of the victims were young women, although the ages of the dead ranged from five months to eighty years.

A memorial to those who died was raised in May 1991 on Talbot Street, where an annual commemoration takes place. Some years later, in 1993, a loyalist paramilitary group, the Ulster Volunteer Force (UVF), claimed responsibility for the bombings. Various unproven allegations state that elements of the British security forces colluded with the UVF in the bombings. No one has ever been charged with the attacks.

ANTI-WAR PROTESTORS

On 15 February 2003, Dublin took its own place in an international protest against a proposed war to be led by the United States against Iraq. Anti-war protests were coordinated during a day of protests in more than 600 cities around the world expressing opposition to the imminent Iraq War.

In Dublin, the march was expected to draw 20,000 people, but in the event so many turned out on a bitterly cold day that both sides of the very wide O'Connell Street were used by the marchers as they streamed through the city in silent protest, many of whom were sporting a new badge designed by Ann Behan, which read 'Just Peace Please'.

Such was the crush of people that the march set off from two sides of Parnell Square, with the head of the procession going to the Department of Foreign Affairs at St Stephen's Green. There were so many people, that the tail of the parade swung into College Green and on up Dame Street, where a truck parked across the junction of South George's Street provided a second platform for speakers. Future President of Ireland, Michael D. Higgins, was among many platform speakers who spoke out against the planned attack.

Estimates about how many people turned out to protest are varied: Garda estimates, always conservative, said there were 80,000 on the streets; the BBC said 90,000; the *Guardian* newspaper said there were 100,000; while the *Socialist Worker* estimated 150,000 people joined the protest. Whatever the numbers, it was certainly enough to disrupt traffic for more than four hours.

However, despite such overwhelming opposition to the war, within a month the 2003 invasion of Iraq had begun. Four countries participated during the initial invasion phase: the United States, United Kingdom, Australia and Poland. A further thirty-six countries were involved in its aftermath.

11

NATURAL HISTORY

IRELAND'S EYE

Ireland's Eye is an island located about 1½km north of Howth in County Dublin. Its Cambrian rocks are made up of quartzite, forming spectacular cliffs on the north-east of the island, which, in turn, provide a sanctuary for seabirds.

In Viking times the island was called Ey – the Viking word for island – but was later changed to Eye. There is a Martello tower at the west end of the island and an ancient, ruined church in the middle. Ironically, the tower was to watch out for later invaders and the church must have seen a few hasty prayers on misty days.

Nowadays, the uninhabited island is home to a rich variety of flora and fauna. The drift soils support a plant community of bracken and various grasses, especially red fescue, along with bluebells, common dog-violet and pennywort. The thinner soils support spring squill, knotted clover and field mouse-ear, and bloody cranesbill has also been recorded. Along the cliffs, you can see rock spurrey, sea stork's bill, rock samphire, golden samphire, sea lavender, meadow rue, portland spurge and tree mallow. There is also a small area of shingle vegetation that occurs above the sandy beach at Carrigeen Bay on the western side of the island, along with curled dock, silverweed and spear-leaved orache, while the rare sea kale, a characteristic species of this habitat, has been known since 1894 and was recorded as recently as 1981.

A variety of seabirds has also been spotted on the island including pairs of fulmar, cormorant, shag, lesser black-backed gull, herring gull, great black-backed gull and kittiwake. Individual peregrine falcons, guillemots and razorbills have also been recorded.

More than enough then to keep any amount of Vikings busy.

HOWTH HEAD

Howth Head is a rocky headland situated on the northern side of Dublin Bay, beloved by walkers and lovers alike. Molly Bloom had her famous soliloquy there in the novel *Ulysses* by Dubliner James Joyce. Of perhaps more pressing interest to nature lovers is that the peninsula is composed of Cambrian slates and quartzites, joined to the mainland by a post glacial raised beach, as many people know.

Howth Head contains both sea cliffs and dry heaths, depending on where you stand to gaze in quiet contemplation. Limestone occurs on the north-west and glacial drift is deposited against the cliffs in places. In open areas, English stonecrop, wood sage and navelwort occur, along with some areas of simple bare rock for rock lovers. Elsewhere, the heath merges into dry grassland with bent grasses, red fescue, cock's-foot, Yorkshire-fog, sweet vernal-grass, lady's bedstraw, ribwort plantain and yellow-wort to be found. In the summit area there are wet flushes and small bogs, where typical bog species such as bog asphodel and sundew may be observed. Patches of scrub, hawthorn, blackthorn, willow and downy birch also occur.

Maritime flora is of particular interest on the Head, which, after all, is surrounded by salt water. A number of scarce and local plants have been recorded, including golden-samphire, sea wormwood, grass-leaved orache, frosted orache, sea spleenwort, bloody crane's-bill, spring squill, sea stork's-bill and three clover species: knotted clover, bird's foot clover and western clover. A number of plant species that are legally protected under a Flora Protection Order have also been recorded on the Head: green-winged orchid, bird's-foot, hairy violet, rough poppy, pennyroyal, heath cudweed and betony. Bird inhabitants include pairs of fulmar, shags, herring gulls, kittiwake, guillemot, and razorbill.

PHOENIX PARK DEER

The fallow deer herd in Phoenix Park numbers around 500 at any given time, with four breeds residing here: black, brown, common and menil. Fallow deer originated in the Mediterranean region about 100,000 years ago, but came to Dublin long after that when the ancestors of the present-day population were brought to Ireland in the thirteenth century by the conquering Normans, who had successfully invaded Ireland in 1169.

Deer moult and shed their coats in spring and autumn, so varieties in colour and shading are best seen in the summer months when the weather is more conducive to deer-spotting. Top bucks begin vocalising around the third week in September, long before the rut begins in mid-October. Gestation takes thirty-three weeks and a single fawn, weighing up to 4kg, is born in the summer of the following year. They lie hidden in long grass until they gain strength. Many are to be found in uncut meadow grass on Fifteen Acres.

During the birthing weeks, warning signs are erected by park staff, in particular asking dog-owners to keep their animals on a leash, as fawns are most vulnerable to attack from dogs and foxes in their early days.

The herd's gene pool is the subject of study both in Ireland and abroad. The mammal research group within University College Dublin's Department of Zoology has conducted detailed and on-going research over many years.

BULL ISLAND

The flat land of Bull Island was formed by the gathering of sand, dating from when the adjacent North Bull Wall was built in 1830, which, along with the Great South Wall, were built to prevent the port of Dublin silting up so that ships could access the port with a degree of certainty. The emerging sand banks interconnected to form a larger whole and over time sand dunes formed on these sand banks from wind action. The dunes are held together by long-rooted marram grass and other sea-hardy plants to form an island that is now a protected nature reserve, golf course and city beach. An extensive salt marsh lies to the north-west and at extreme low tides there are extensive mud flats visible between the island and the mainland.

Bull Island Interpretative Centre enables visitors to learn more about the island's unique flora and fauna and the specialised habitats of the surrounding sand dunes and salt marshes.

The reserves of Bull Island – which was declared an UNESCO Biosphere in 1981 and a National Nature Reserve in 1988 – are of international scientific importance for Brent Geese and for botanical, ornithological, zoological and geomorphological species that grow there.

GLENASMOLE

Glenasmole Valley lies on the edge of the Wicklow uplands, with the River Dodder flowing through it. It forms two reservoirs, which supply water to south Dublin, and contains examples of calcareous fen and flush areas. The non-calcareous bedrock of Glenasmole Valley has been overlain by deep drift deposits, which now line the valley sides. They are partly covered by scrub and woodland and, on the less precipitous parts, by a herb-rich grassland. There is much seepage through the deposits, that brings to the surface water rich in bases, which induces local patches of calcareous fen and, in places, petrifying springs. Glenasmole is a priority habitat listed on Annex I of the EU Habitats Directive.

Orchid-rich grassland occurs in the drier parts of the valley. Species recorded include frog orchid, northern marsh-orchid, fragrant orchid, marsh helleborine, early-purple orchid and greater butterfly orchid. Also found in Glenasmole are green-winged orchid and small-white orchid. The sward includes sweet vernal-grass, creeping bent and crested dog's-tail. Other species occurring are common bird's-foot-trefoil, kidney vetch, common restharrow, yellow-wort and autumn gentian.

A hazel wood has developed on the unstable calcareous slopes and includes ash, downy birch, goat willow and whitebeam. Spring wood-rush, wood speedwell and brambles are included in the ground flora. Wet semi-natural broad-leaved woodland is found around the reservoirs and includes alder and willow. Glenasmole provides excellent habitat for bat species, with pipistrelle, leisler's, daubenton's and brown long-eared bat recorded. Otters occur along the river and reservoirs.

A perfect setting then for mythological stories of Fionn Mac Cumhaill and the Fianna, who are said to have roamed the area, long, long, ago.

BOOTERSTOWN MARSH

The Booterstown Marsh Nature Reserve, located between the coastal railway line and the Rock Road, is a 4-hectare water marsh that can be seen from the public road by the sea. An area of salt marsh and muds, with brackish water, it includes the only salt marsh and bird sanctuary in south Dublin Bay.

There are three main habitats ranging from near-freshwater in the north-western corner to near-saltwater by the DART station, with a graduation between.

Flora present includes the salt-
tolerant species of sea milkwort,
false fox sedge, and sea
spurrey. Birds may be seen
in large numbers at the
reserve: the marsh area attracts
moorhen, common teal, reed bunting,
coot, mallard duck, sedge warbler,
common snipe, little egret, northern
lapwing, eurasian oystercatcher, bar-
tailed godwit, common redshank, dunlin,
knot, and brent goose. Other species
breeding in the marsh or visiting from nearby
breeding locations include common blackbird, dunnock and wren.
Rarer visitors to the reserve are grey heron, spotted redshank, ruff and
little stint. Kingfisher, greenshank and water rail are seen in the south-
eastern corner, while from the sea and shore common gull, herring gull
and black-headed gull sweep in to create an unceasing vista of nature.

12

STORY AND PAGE

ONE CITY ONE BOOK

Each year Dublin city council encourages people to read a book connected with the capital city during the month of April. The reading series began in 2006 when *At Swim-Two-Birds* by Flann O'Brien was the chosen title for that year, even though O'Brien was born in Tyrone. However, he did graduate from University College Dublin and *At Swim-Two-Birds* mixes Irish history and legend with a profound knowledge of Dublin's streets, bars and urban life. Each year after that saw a different title being chosen:

2007: *A Long Long Way* by Dubliner Sebastian Barry, about the First World War, which was not in Dublin.

2008: *Gulliver's Travels* by Jonathan Swift, who was Dean of St Patrick's Cathedral.

2009: *Dracula* by Bram Stoker became the chill of the year. Stoker hailed from Clontarf where the Irish chieftain Brian Boru was killed in battle one Good Friday, a long time before Stoker cleared his throat for the first time.

2010: *The Picture of Dorian Gray* by Oscar Wilde. This was Wilde's only published novel and explores the many interrelationships between art, life and consequence.

2011: *Ghost Light* by Joseph O'Connor, whose family hail from the Liberties, was the book to be seen reading in public around Dublin. It is loosely based on a love affair between the playwright John Millington Synge and the Abbey Theatre actress Molly Allgood, both now dead.

2012: the entire city was being encouraged to read *Dubliners* by James Joyce, a short-story collection published before his more famous *Ulysses* and *Finnegan's Wake*.

2013: *Strumpet City* by James Plunkett, set during the period of the 1913 Lockout, whose centenary was the same year.

2014: the newly written *If Ever You Go: A Map of Dublin in Poetry and Song* by Pat Boran and Gerard Smyth.

IRISH NATIONAL ANTHEM AND THE RED FLAG

Writer Brendan Behan once said the first thing on the agenda for any new organisation would be the Split. Accordingly, in June 1923, the Dublin newspaper the *Mail* ran a competition to select an Irish national anthem, even though Amhrán na bhFiann (The Soldiers Song) was already being used informally, but, the important thing was that it had not been adopted formally. The paper appointed W.B. Yeats, Lennox Robinson and James Stephens to adjudicate in a competition for a new anthem, with a prize of 50 guineas on offer for the winning ditty. However, the adjudicators, having mulled the thing over between them, decided that none of the new compositions were of sufficient standard to win the prize and that was that.

Five years later, in 1928, the Irish Free State adopted Amhrán na bhFiann as its anthem, which it has been ever since. The music was composed by Peadar Kearney and Patrick Heeney and the original English lyrics are by Kearney, with the Irish language translation by Liam Ó Rinn. Purely by coincidence, Kearney was Brendan Behan's Uncle Peadar and Peadar's sister Kathleen was Brendan's mammy. Peadar started his working life as a Dublin housepainter, but is now remembered for his songs.

Meanwhile, a Dublin docker called Jim Connell, who was born in County Meath in 1852, wrote the Red Flag, the socialist anthem. Connell was awarded the Red Star Medal by Vladimir Lenin in 1922, proving that a good tune will travel anywhere and last for a long time, 50 guineas or no 50 guineas.

BRAM STOKER

Dublin is a great place for festivals, which in Dublin means meeting a lot of people and having as much fun and conversation as is possible, given the prescribed number of hours there are in any one day or night.

The Bram Stoker Festival runs at the end of October and coincides with the final long weekend of the Irish calendar, before everyone gets ready for Christmas. Dublin City inhabitants and their camp followers are encouraged to celebrate the life, work and legacy of Bram Stoker and his gothic novel *Dracula*, a book that has never been out of print since it was published in 1897.

On 4 December 1878, long before the book saw the light of day, St Ann's Church on Dawson Street was the venue for the marriage of Bram Stoker to Florence Balcombe, who had previously been keeping company with Oscar Wilde, which goes to show that the woman liked a challenge, and a bit of a thrill. During his lifetime, Stoker was better known as personal assistant to the actor Henry Irving and business manager of the Lyceum Theatre in London, which Irving owned. While earning a crust with Irving and the Lyceum Theatre, Stoker began writing novels, among which was *Dracula*.

Dublin writer Sheridan Le Fanu's *Carmilla* predates *Dracula* by twenty-five years. *Carmilla* is a Gothic novella that tells the story of a young woman's susceptibility to the attentions of a female vampire; it seems Stoker may have read *Carmilla* before he penned *Dracula*. He also visited the crypt of St Michan's Church on Church Street to view the scattered mummies lying outside their coffins for all to see.

Dracula is written as a collection of realistic, but completely fictional, diary entries, telegrams, letters, ship's logs and newspaper clippings, all of which added a level of detailed realism to his story – a skill Stoker developed as a newspaper writer.

After suffering a number of strokes, Stoker died on 20 April 1912, five days after the *Titanic* sank with so many lost souls aboard, though the events were unrelated. His wife, Florence Balcombe, died many years later in 1937 at the age of 78.

NEWSPAPERS

The *Dublin Evening Mail* was launched in 1823. It proved to be the longest lasting evening paper in Ireland, only closing down in 1962 when it lost a three-way battle for Dublin evening readers with the *Evening Herald* and the cocky new *Evening Press*, even though as recently as the early 1950s it had been Dublin's biggest selling evening newspaper.

However, the paper's circulation did go up and down during the century. During the Land War of the nineteenth century it took a pro-landlord position and compared the Land League (which was then agitating for land ownership reform) to the Mafia and the Colorado beetle and demanded that Ireland be subjected to martial law. Not surprisingly, its readership in 1900 was small compared with national papers such as the *Evening Telegraph*, *The Irish Times*, and the *Freeman's Journal*. Nevertheless it managed to outlast both the *Telegraph* and the *Freeman's Journal*, but faced a stiffer challenge in the mid-twentieth century from the *Evening Herald* and *Evening Press*.

The Irish Times bought the *Mail* in its final few years, but the new owner closed the paper on 10 July 1962 and several of its staff and columns transferred directly over to *The Irish Times*. The *Evening Press* closed down in 1995, leaving the *Dublin Evening Herald* the final survivor of the three. In 2013, the survivor was renamed and re-branded as the *Herald* and marketed as a morning paper.

On the literary front, the *Dublin Evening Mail* featured in short stories in James Joyce's *The Dubliners*. The *Mail* was once co-owned by author Sheridan Le Fanu. Bram Stoker, author of *Dracula*, worked as an unpaid theatre critic for the paper.

BOB GELDOF

Bob Geldof is a Dublin-born singer, songwriter, author and political activist. He was the lead singer of the Boomtown Rats in the late 1970s and early 1980s, a band that had some success during the punk rock era.

His number one single in the UK, 'I Don't Like Mondays', was written in the aftermath of a shooting spree by 16-year-old Brenda Ann Spencer, who fired at children in a school playground at Grover Cleveland Elementary School in San Diego, California on 29 January 1979, killing two adults and injuring eight children and one police officer. Spencer said afterwards she did so because she did not like Mondays. Geldof also co-wrote 'Do They Know It's Christmas', one of the best-selling singles of all time, in response to starvation in Africa.

In 1984 he and Midge Ure founded the charity Band Aid to raise money for famine relief in Ethiopia. The pair went on to organise Live Aid the following year and the Live 8 concerts in 2005. Live Aid was a dual-venue concert held on 13 July 1985 to raise funds for relief of the on-going Ethiopian famine. It was held simultaneously at Wembley Stadium in London, attended by 72,000 people, and John F. Kennedy Stadium in Philadelphia, attended by some 100,000 people. An estimated global audience of 1.9 billion across 150 nations watched the live broadcast, making it one of the largest-scale satellite link-ups and television broadcasts of all time.

Geldof has been nominated for the Nobel Peace Prize, was granted an honorary knighthood by Queen Elizabeth II and is a recipient of the Man of Peace title. He was made a freeman of his native Dublin in March 2006.

BONO

Dubliner Bono was born Paul David Hewson. His stage name comes from Bono Vox, an alteration of Bonavox, which translates as good voice. Incidentally, there was a hearing aid company in Dublin that used the Bonavox brand name, but they were not singers, as far as is known.

Bono was frontman for the Dublin-based rock band U2, which performed all over the world, as well as in Dublin. He attended

Mount Temple Comprehensive School, where he met his future wife, Alison Stewart, and the future members of U2, which was good.

Bono wrote almost all U2's lyrics and they sold lots of records and appeared in many places in front of many people. Outside the band, the singer collaborated and recorded with numerous other artists.

As Hewson/Bono he was praised and criticised alike for his activism and involvement with U2, proving that it is hard to please everyone, all the time.

Bono and fellow band members were granted the Freedom of the City of Dublin by the city council in 2000, which was also good.

The Edge, Larry Mullen Junior, Adam Clayton and the band's manager Paul McGuinness, were all honoured by Dublin. Their names were entered on a roll of free men of the city that dates back to Isaac Butt, in 1876, though he was dead before Bono recorded his first songs.

Bono was nominated for the Nobel Peace Prize, was granted a knighthood by Queen Elizabeth II of the United Kingdom, though he was not a British citizen, and, with Bill and Melinda Gates, was named Time Person of the Year in 2005. In 2013, Bono was made a Commandeur of the French Ordre des Arts et des Lettres.

THE DUBLINERS

The Dubliners were founded in Dublin in 1962, more or less. The folk group started off as The Ronnie Drew Ballad Group and used to play as an interval act in Dublin theatres. It changed names when Luke Kelly suggested they call it The Dubliners after James Joyce's book of the same name, which Kelly was reading at the time. Its founding members were Ronnie Drew (Spanish guitar), Luke Kelly (five-string banjo), Barney McKenna (nineteen-fret tenor banjo) and Ciaran Bourke (guitar, tin whistle and harmonica), later joined by John Sheehan (violin), all bearded men, forming the core group in a shifting line-up over the years.

They achieved success in their own town first and then throughout the rest of the country and abroad, liked for their mix of Irish folk songs, traditional street ballads, protest songs and instrumentals. Bizarrely, they even appeared on *Top of the Pops* in 1967, with chart hits of their recordings of traditional folk songs

'Seven Drunken Nights' and 'Black Velvet Band'. Collaborations with The Pogues in 1987 saw them enter the UK Singles Chart on a further two occasions.

The versions of folk songs sung by Ronnie Drew and Luke Kelly tended to be become definitive versions. Kelly's version of 'Raglan Road' is considered a litmus test by Dublin audiences whenever another singer attempts the song; few succeed in the challenge.

The Dubliners celebrated fifty years together in 2012, but announced their retirement in the autumn of that year, following the passing of founding member Barney McKenna. Ciaran Bourke had passed away in 1988; Luke Kelly in 1984 and Ronnie Drew in 2008, but their influence on Irish folk music continues as strong as ever.

STRUMPET CITY

Strumpet City, James Plunkett's novel of Dublin life at the time of the 1913 Lockout, was published in 1969 and went on to sell a quarter of a million copies in more than a dozen languages. RTE's

1980 dramatisation of the book, scripted by Hugh Leonard, was sold to more than thirty countries. Furthermore, it was chosen as the book for Dubliners to read in the One City One Book promotion for 2013 and sold even more copies in the centenary year of its setting.

The novel follows the lives of a dozen characters as they are swept up in the tumultuous events that affected Dublin between 1907, when Edward VII arrived for a visit, and concludes as the First World War opens in 1914.

Its author, born in 1920 in Dublin's inner city, was the son of a First World War veteran who was a member of Jim Larkin's Irish Transport and General Workers Union. His background had a life-long impact on James Plunkett Kelly, who shortened his pen name to James Plunkett. Plunkett worked as a clerk in the Dublin Gas Company and later joined the trade union movement, serving under Larkin between 1946 and 1947. In 1955 he joined the permanent staff of Radió Éireann, as assistant head of drama and variety.

Plunkett wrote numerous plays and novels, including *Farewell Companions* and *The Circus Animals*. He once said he wrote from persistent memories, which he wanted to write down in order to exorcise them. Plunkett passed away in a Dublin nursing home, aged 82, in 2003.

BRIDGES OF DUBLIN

Over the years, many bridges have been built over the River Liffey in Dublin, several of which have been rebuilt and renamed according to the shifting patterns of power through the years. Here they all are, from east to west (dates given are the earliest dates for a bridge crossing at this point):

East-Link Bridge: first tolled drawbridge in modern times, East Wall Road to York Road (1987)

Samuel Beckett Bridge: road bridge, Guild Street to Sir John Rogerson's Quay (2009)

Seán O'Casey Bridge: footbridge, Sir John Rogerson's Quay to North Wall Quay (2005)

Talbot Memorial Bridge: road bridge, Memorial Road to Moss Street (1978)

Loopline Bridge: railbridge, with overhead power supply for DART line (1891)

Butt Bridge: road bridge, Beresford Place to Tara Street (1932)

Rosie Hackett Bridge: public transport bridge, Marlborough Street to Hawkins Street (2014)

O'Connell Bridge: road bridge, O'Connell Street Lower to Westmoreland Street and D'Olier Street (1791)

Liffey Bridge/Ha'penny Bridge/Metal Bridge: footbridge, Liffey Street Lower to Merchant's Arch (1816)

Millennium Bridge: footbridge, Ormonde Quay to Wellington Quay (1999)

Grattan Bridge/Essex Bridge/Capel Street Bridge: road bridge, Capel Street to Parliament Street (1676)

O'Donovan Rossa Bridge/Richmond Bridge/Ormond Bridge: road bridge, Chancery Place to Winetavern Street (1684)

Father Mathew Bridge/Whitworth Bridge/Old Bridge: road bridge, Church Street to Bridge Street Lower (1014)

Mellowes Bridge/Queen's Bridge/Queen Maeve Bridge: road bridge, Queen Street to Bridgefoot Street (1683)

James Joyce Bridge: road bridge, Blackhall Place to Ushers Island (2003)

Rory O'More Bridge/Victoria and Albert Bridge/Queen Victoria Bridge: road bridge, Watling Street to Ellis Street (1670)

Frank Sherwin Bridge: road bridge, St John's Road West to Wolfe Tone Quay (1981)

Seán Heuston Bridge/King's Bridge/Sarsfield Bridge: light rail and footbridge, Heuston station to Wolfe Tone Quay (1828)

Liffey Railway Bridge: rail freight bridge, Heuston Station to Phoenix Park Tunnel (1877)

Sarah or Sarah's Bridge: road bridge, South Circular Road to Conyngham Road at Islandbridge (1577)

Anna Livia Bridge/Chapelizod Bridge: road bridge, Lucan Road to Chapelizod Road (1660s)

Farmleigh Bridge: disused service bridge, Farmleigh House (1850s)

West-Link Bridge: tolled road bridge, M50 motorway (1990)

Lucan Bridge: Lower Lucan Road (1200s)

www.bridgesofdublin.ie

OTHER DUBLINS

USA

Dublin, Montgomery, Alabama

Dublin, Graham, Arizona

Dublin, Logan, Arkansas

Dublin, Alameda, California

Dublin, Bladen, North Carolina

Dublin, Lake, Florida

Dublin, Laurens, Georgia

Dublin, Wayne, Indiana

Dublin, Graves, Kentucky

Dublin, Maine

Dublin, Harford, Maryland

Dublin, Manistee, Michigan

Dublin, Coahoma, Mississippi

Dublin, Cheshire, New Hampshire

Dublin, Paterson, New Jersey

Dublin, Seneca, New York

Dublin, North Carolina

Dublin, Franklin, Ohio

Dublin, Mahoning, Ohio

Dublin, Bucks, Pennsylvania

Dublin, Fulton, Pennsylvania

Dublin, Huntingdon, Pennsylvania

Dublin, Erath, Texas

Dublin, Pulaski, Virginia

Australia

Dublin, South Australia

Canada

Dublin, Ontario

If you enjoyed this book, you may also be interested in…

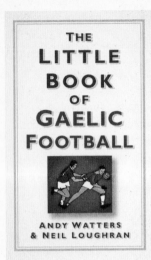

The Little Book of Gaelic Football

ANDY WATTERS & NEIL LOUGHRAN

Fact-packed and light-hearted in style, this reliable reference book and quirky guide reveals little-known facts about Gaelic football along with details of classic matches, statistical records, famous players, amusing anecdotes, and a general history. This can be dipped into time and time again to reveal something new about this ancient game.

978 1 84588 806 0

The Little Book of Ireland

C.M. BOYLAN

A reliable reference book and a quirky guide, this can be dipped into time and time again to reveal something new about the people, the heritage, the secrets and the enduring fascination of this ancient country. Despite being a relatively small island on the edge of the vast Atlantic there is always something new, charming, or even bizarre to discover about the Emerald Isle – and you will find much of it here.

978 1 84588 804 6